Applied Improvisation for Coaches and Leaders

Leadership, teamwork, creativity, and storytelling are hot topics in contemporary training and management. They are also an integral part of applied improvisation, which as a result gives us a valuable stock of exercises and methods to impart these skills. In *Applied Improvisation for Coaches and Leaders: A Practical Guide for Creative Collaboration*, Schinko-Fischli provides a complete introduction to applying the principles and techniques of improvisational theatre to working life.

Schinko-Fischli uses her wealth of experience to illuminate how trainers and managers can add new stimuli to their work through applied improvisation. The book begins with a general introduction to the development of improvisational theatre and to applied improvisation, defining the foundations of improvisation and how we can usefully apply these methods to teamwork. It then focuses on how we can use creativity, with a particular focus on co-creativity, to pave the way for new visions of the future and innovative solutions, and explores how storytelling can be applied to teamwork and presentations. Finally, Schinko-Fischli examines status, looking at how we present ourselves and appear to others, and how we can influence and control this. This unique book takes a fresh and nuanced look at many soft skills and presents a complete overview of the areas in which applied improvisation may be used by coaches and managers. It contains practical exercises throughout and clearly explains relevant theory and terminology.

Applied Improvisation for Coaches and Leaders: A Practical Guide for Creative Collaboration will be essential reading for coaches in practice and in training, particularly executive coaches, and those who work with leaders in teams and organizations. It will also be a key text for leaders, trainers and managers seeking to enhance and expand their soft skills and make learning gainful and enjoyable.

Susanne Schinko-Fischli is a freelance trainer based in Switzerland who focuses on communication, group dynamics, team development, creativity, presentation techniques, and competence in self-presentation. She is a teaching trainer for group dynamics at the Austrian Society for Group Dynamics and Organisational Consulting and lecturer at the Universities of Liechtenstein, Linz and Graz, and at the Zurich University of Applied Sciences. She has given workshops using applied improvisation at the ETH, Zurich, and has worked for companies such as IBM.

Applied Improvisation for Coaches and Leaders

A Practical Guide for Creative
Collaboration

Susanne Schinko-Fischli

Routledge
Taylor & Francis Group

LONDON AND NEW YORK

First published 2019
by Routledge
2 Park Square, Milton Park, Abingdon, Oxon OX14 4RN

and by Routledge
52 Vanderbilt Avenue, New York, NY 10017

Routledge is an imprint of the Taylor & Francis Group, an informa business

First published in **German** under the title *Angewandte Improvisation für Coaches und Führungskräfte* by **Susanne Schinko-Fischli**

Copyright © **2018, Springer-Verlag GmbH Deutschland**

This edition has been translated and published under licence from **Springer-Verlag GmbH, DE.**

© 2019 Susanne Schinko-Fischli

British Library Cataloguing-in-Publication Data
A catalogue record for this book is available from the British Library

Library of Congress Cataloging-in-Publication Data
A catalog record for this book has been requested

ISBN: 978-1-138-31524-2 (hbk)
ISBN: 978-1-138-31526-6 (pbk)
ISBN: 978-0-429-45647-3 (ebk)

Typeset in Times New Roman
by Apex CoVantage, LLC

Translated by John Newman

Contents

Preface

At the time this book is published, we see a United States president whose erratic, unpredictable and – in his eyes at least – effective behaviour may possibly be interpreted as gifted improvisation. However, the characteristics of improvisation that Susanne Schinko-Fischli vividly and systematically lays out in this book allow no such interpretation. Only improvisation as it is described in these pages can contribute to the success of the group, the team, the organization, and the nation, whereas self-obsessed delusions strengthen nothing more than an individual's ego.

With its comprehensive feature lists and exercises that can be directly applied, Susanne Schinko-Fischli's book is a "must" for trainers and coaches wishing to let individuals, teams, and companies get to know something about improvisation, creative behaviour, or simply artful coordination. Reading this book reminds us how fruitful the principles of improvisation offered here can be for leaders, precisely because they are set against many of the management practices that are dominant today. Although leaders like to refer to what they do as an "art" that goes beyond the rules learned in university and seminars, they tend to see improvisation as a last resort to fall back on when their precious rules fall short. Improvisation, though, is an art. Susanne Schinko-Fischli shows us that this art is not only for the theatre, but also for daily life.

We love to say, "the way is the goal." In reality we have come to accept as normal and natural the fact that in our society only the product – or even only the profit made from it – is rewarded, while the process leading to it is of no importance whatsoever. If we were to focus instead on the process and artful improvisation, what changes would be involved? How radically fresh would meetings look if all participants were expected to "make their partner look good?" How differently would managers act if they were not personally shielded from risk, but rather were prepared to "fail with good humour" in front of their colleagues, and genuinely "see mistakes as an essential source of creativity," "allow themselves to be changed by their colleagues," and now and then break with routines. Managers should let themselves be carried away by this book!

While in a few years a new United States president will take the helm – possibly a genuine master of the art of improvisation – we will still happily reach for this book for inspiration. And I hope and trust there will be a great many of us readers doing so.

Linz, in summer 2017
Johannes M. Lehner
Professor at the Institute for Organisation,
Johannes Kepler University Linz

Foreword

I always wanted to be an actress, and after a successful career at Vienna's Burg-theater and appearances on all the improvisational theatre stages of this world, I decided to pass on my knowledge and experience, so now I work with applied improvisation.

OK, so my life did not work out quite that smoothly. And if it had indeed worked out like that, then I would not have had any interesting stories to tell (see "Storytelling" chapter). As a child, I never wanted to be an actress; I would never have thought myself capable. At 14 I started looking into psychology and wanting to become a psychotherapist, and I did indeed go on to study psychology.

During my studies a friend introduced me to acting, and I became a little less interested in psychology; from then on I only wanted to be an actress. I went to stage school, continuing my psychology studies on the side. But my glittering career as an actress was not to be, as I simply did not have enough talent. Instead, I discovered an even greater passion: "improv theatre." But this love was also unrequited. Yes, I trained for a long time and with many different improv groups and teachers, and gave many performances, but on this stage too I would never be "good enough" to build a wonderful career. I had many setbacks, but also many unforgettable nights and emotional flights of fancy . . .

After my psychology degree I started working; after all, I still had to earn money. But I remained passionate about theatre, and I never stopped hoping to make a living out of it. In my first "real" job, being with my colleagues sparked my second great love: group dynamics. Then, through ÖGGO, the Austrian Society for Group Dynamics and Organisational Consulting, I met the love of my (private) life, my husband.

It was already clear that I would not be successful enough as an actress to make a living out of it. But it was also clear that improv theatre would always be part of my life. So I started combining this with my profession by offering Train-the-Trainer Workshops, using methods from improvisational theatre. This worked well right from the start, and for the first time I felt at home in my professional life. It was not long before I became more independent as a trainer, increasingly bringing improvisational theatre into my seminars. Back in 2002 this was all new in Europe; improvisational theatre in this form had only recently come to Vienna, and applied improvisation itself was only two years old, and hardly known at all. It was many years later that I happened to come across the Applied Improvisation Network, and realized that this was exactly what I had been doing all along.

During my time as an independent trainer I could see that I was in the right place, because I was finally receiving the positive feedback I had hoped for (not always, but mostly), and because I was getting more and more assignments. I have come to recognize that my strength lies in the very fact that I am NOT a born actress, which means that from my own experience I can feel the fears, uncertainties, doubts, and difficulties of the participants in my workshops.

What is important in my life, and what has helped me in many situations, are the basic principles of improvisation:

Accepting offers ("Yes, and...").
I have always been open to new and unknown things, which has let me find out what I really enjoy and where my talents are.

Having ideas, and letting them go again.
I have had many ideas and dreams, not all of which have come to fruition. But I have been able to let them go, and remain open to what comes next.

Successful failure.
Yes, I have often failed, and I made many mistakes, yet I am still doing exactly what I most want to do – or maybe it is those very mistakes that allow me to do it.

The core theme of this book is how we can apply the principles and methods from improvisational theatre to leadership and management, in training sessions, and in our personal lives. I begin the book with a general introduction to improvisational theatre and applied improvisation. I then describe the foundations of improvisation and how these methods can be deployed in teamwork. Another chapter looks at creativity, with a particular focus on co-creativity. The chapter on status is not about status symbols, but about the status we assume in the way we present ourselves, and how we can influence that. Storytelling is now a hot topic in companies, and I look at how stories are built up, and how we can implement storytelling in teamwork and presentations. Improvisational theatre offers many methods and exercises relating to how we present ourselves. These can enhance every appearance and presentation, as described in the last chapter.

Most chapters end with a collection of exercises, with much talk of "players" and the "stage." By "players" I mean the seminar participants doing the exercises. The "stage" is simply the open space in front of the "audience" (the seminar participants). The exercises are suitable for groups of 6–14 participants. Some exercises are also suitable for large groups. Unfortunately, I am no longer able to re-trace the origins and creators of the exercises; I learned them in workshops or from other improv groups, read about them in specialist literature, or invented them myself. Most of the exercises have been common on the improv scene for a long time, and have also been adapted over the years. Many exercises go back to the past masters such as Viola Spolin or Keith Johnstone.

Applied improvisation works on the principles of leading and allowing oneself to be led. Through its playful process, it generates creative and "co-creative" events, and thus new shared images of the future, and innovative solutions. This shows us that our own status as a key foundation of all our communication is not something that we have, but something that we do, and which we can influence.

This book is aimed at coaches, trainers, and managers seeking new inspiration for their work. The methods of applied improvisation offer a wholly new perspective on many of the so-called soft skills. For the sake of readability, this book uses either masculine or feminine forms at different points, as appropriate.

In creating this book, I wish to give my heartfelt thanks to my husband Claudius Fischli. He always supported me in my plan, he gave me the time I needed to do it at all, he read many of the chapters, and gave me vital feedback on them!

I also wish to thank Annemarie Mitterhofer, who assisted me with many aspects of the book, and helped me find an illustrator.

My thanks go out to Evi Fill, whose talent as an artist transformed my descriptions and examples into such effective and appropriate illustrations.

And I would also like to thank Susannah Frearson at Routledge for looking after me so well, from the start of the book right to the end.

And of course to John Newman for the excellent translation into English!

Appenzell, in spring 2018
Susanne Schinko-Fischli

Portraits

About the author

Susanne Schinko-Fischli was born in Vienna in 1972, and studied psychology at the University of Vienna and at the University of California, San Diego. Alongside those studies she trained as an actress and as a professional trainer for group dynamics. She has appeared many times on stage with a variety of improvisational theatre groups in Austria and Switzerland. Since 2004 she has been a freelance trainer focusing on her passion: the vibrant methods and dynamics of applied improvisation. Susanne Schinko-Fischli is a lecturer at the University of Liechtenstein and University of Graz, at the Zurich University of Applied Sciences, and at colleges and polytechnics. As a trainer in social competence, teamwork, and innovation, she works with renowned organizations in Switzerland, Austria, Germany, and the English-speaking world.

Susanne Schinko-Fischli

About the illustrator

Evi Fill (Filluna) was actually a graphic designer, but whenever she ran out of images to work on, she would draw them herself. Eventually her drawing and painting took over entirely. But her heart is still in advertising, so 95 per cent of her work is for Austrian, Swiss, and German advertising agencies, for whom she most enjoys creating storyboards and layout illustrations. In that line of work she can find herself in the role of director, stylist, and location scout, discovering small worlds, populating them with actors, and operating the camera. Over time she added vector work, classical illustration, characters,

Evi Fill (Filluna)

and a range of styles and images for every occasion to her repertoire, and became something of a maid-of-all-work. After 15 years this automatically led to her being given perhaps the last-ever employee position as an illustrator. She has now been freelance since 2011, and is enjoying her new challenges.

Chapter 1

Improvisational theatre

Introduction to improvisational theatre

"Homo improvicus"

Although unforeseen events are part of daily life, we have an ambivalent attitude towards them, as they remind us that we cannot plan anything in our lives perfectly, that we never know just what the future will bring, and that in the end we will never have control over our existence. This unsettles us.

At the same time, this unpredictability offers us many opportunities. The Latin word "improvus" means both "unforeseen" and "surprise." It is not for nothing that neuropsychologists have discovered that little stimulates the reward centres in our brain more than a pleasant surprise. Marketers and media strategists will often exploit this. Our ability to react spontaneously to unforeseen events is part of our make-up as humans, which we have inherited from our stone-age ancestors. If they happened to come across a bison, they had to be capable of killing it on the spot and taking it to a safe place before others were able to take the valuable food away. It would have been unproductive for stone-age people to have been too bound up with their root-gathering habits to make the most of such surprising discoveries.

Figure 1.1 © Evi Fill

Still, the double-edged character of the unexpected remains a "problem" for us humans. In our globalized world, with our strict timetables and our days that seem full to the brim without a second to spare, surprises are a nuisance to us – even those that should be positive. On the way to the kindergarten, where we have to drop our child before work, the bus or tram has to be right there at the stop at the exact moment shown in our public transport app. To gaze at the unexpectedly beautiful morning sky, or to bump into an acquaintance and chat with them a while, is out of the question.

This is why sectors have arisen dealing with the predictability of events, with hosts of professions attempting to master this art. This works relatively well in some domains (e.g. weather forecasting), and less well in others (such as predicting elections in recent times). The fact is that, despite all the effort we invest in trying, the future remains unplannable.

Improvisation is one solution to this "problem," as in a certain way it hands us back the reins. If we can catch the ball that fate has suddenly thrown at us, we can focus on a new goal, and this goal may be beneficial to us. If we allow it, something new may emerge.

We have to improvise whenever something happens that throws our plans into disarray, and when we have to re-plan the future, such as when we are developing new and innovative products or services. Here, improvisation methods are increasingly being put to use, as new horizons can only be opened up through the openness that improvisation makes possible. But how should we improvise "correctly"? To answer this, we need to look to art, as art might be said to have improvisation in its DNA. Theatre, music, dance, and literature would be unthinkable without the artists' ability to improvise. For a long time, improvisational theatre has concerned itself, both practically and theoretically, with the basic principles of improvising, how to communicate and improvise effectively within teams, and thus how to nurture creativity together!

Origins of improvisational theatre

Improvisation in theatre has a rather chequered past. It was present from the very earliest days of theatre, precisely because it was not yet possible to plan everything. It was not until late antiquity that scripts and movements became formalized and fixed, and from that time onwards improvisation was gradually forced out of the theatre. Only with the birth of the commedia dell'arte in Italy was it able to blossom once more. Here, improvisation was used to criticize the political realm, and to poke fun at society. The growth in censorship in the 18th century saw unscripted theatre, and improvisation with it, sidelined again. In the 20th century Jacob Levy Moreno breathed fresh life into it, allowing it finally to return for good. From this time, new forms of improvisational theatre emerged, and Keith Johnstone's

Theatresports spread quickly from Canada to the United States, and later to Europe. Since the start of the 21st century, Theatresports and other styles of improvisational theatre have become very popular in many countries around the world.

It all began with mimetic performances:

Mime

The origins of theatre lie in occult rituals and ceremonies, whereby performers usually depicted a hoped-for situation; for example, hunters may have imitated the animals they caught. In antiquity, mime was developed from these rituals, and gradually lost its religious significance. The term "mime" comes from the Latin for "imitator." Mimesis involves embodying and imitating real-life people, and given that in early theatre much was still unplanned and had to be improvised, these performances were closely bound up with improvisation right from the start. This form of theatre dominated Greek and Roman stages until late antiquity, until scripts and movements started to become more rigidly fixed.

It was not until the 16th century that improvisation in theatre started to regain significance, in the form of the commedia dell'arte.

Commedia dell'arte

In the 16th century the commedia dell'arte was a milestone in theatre, and particularly in improvisational theatre. This style emerged in northern Italy, and harked back to the buffoonery of ancient Rome and the carnival performances of Venice. Each actor had a fixed character (mask), who he portrayed his whole life. The roles and the dramatic context were established, but the plot was improvised. As there were no written dialogues, the actors were free to represent the views of the lower classes, and thus criticize society without immediately having to deal with censorship.

The commedia dell'arte was also known as "commedia improvvisa," and helped improvisation become an established art form. It strongly influenced authors such as Brecht, Giorgio Strehler, and Dario Fo, and the old Viennese Volkstheater (People's Theatre) of the 19th century. The commedia dell'arte also gave rise to the Stegreiftheater (improvised theatre), which wandering players took with great success all over Europe.

Stegreiftheater

Stegreiftheater is an early form of modern improvisational theatre. The word Stegreif comes from Middle High German, and means stirrup. As in the commedia dell'arte, in Stegreiftheater the characters and scenes are fixed, but the dialogues are improvised by the players, a technique also known as extemporization. Extempore phrases, or even songs, are created "on the spur of the moment," and often driven by the audience. When the actors could extemporize well – that is, improvise – audiences very much appreciated it. However, authors and above all censors feared it and fought against it.

From the middle of the 18th century, censorship required scripts to be fixed, and the popularity of commedia dell'arte and Stegreiftheater gradually waned. In 1752 in Vienna, an adviser to Maria Theresa implemented a ban on extemporization, thus sounding the death knell of the Stegreiftheater in Austria. From then on, theatre was to depict bourgeois life, with great importance given to training and instruction. The year 1836 saw Johann Nepomuk Nestroy banned from the stage for extemporization, and he even spent a short time in prison. Only in the 20th century did Stegreiftheater once again gain a foothold.

Jacob Levy Moreno's psychodrama

In 1921, Jacob Levy Moreno founded a Stegreiftheater in Vienna, and experimented with improvisation there. He was particularly fascinated by the vitality and immediacy of Stegreiftheater. In Vienna, and later in the USA, he developed it into method of psychotherapy. He aimed to get people to act spontaneously and creatively to help free them from their rigid roles and behaviour patterns. Thus, he developed the "psychodrama" form of psychotherapy, which had originally been conceived as an action-oriented alternative to psychoanalysis.

Jakob Levy Moreno also created the book "Das Stegreiftheater" (1924), which was the first to deal with theoretical concepts of improvisation. Today, psychodrama is principally used as a form of group therapy, whereby conflicts, for example, are resolved by an improvised exchange of roles.

Viola Spolin

The acting coach and author Viola Spolin first studied under the sociologist Neva Boyd in her Group Work School in Chicago, receiving training in the leadership of groups, the use of leisure time, and social work. She was particularly inspired to see how traditional structures of acting could be used to adapt the social behaviour of children from immigrant and socially disadvantaged families.

In 1946, Spolin founded the Young Actors Company in Hollywood, giving acting training to children, and experimenting with a variety of improvisational theatre techniques. With her methods, she wanted to help her pupils remain focused in the moment and to make improvised decisions on stage that echoed real life. To achieve this, Spolin developed playful exercises to facilitate the creative process.

These theatre games transformed complicated theatrical conventions into simple forms of acting, whereby each piece had a specific focus. Of these, Spolin laid particular emphasis on concentration. To nurture this, she would focus on an acting assignment such as working with a prop (and later also working on a character or on a feeling). This focus on one detail aimed to prevent the pupils becoming overwhelmed or fearful. By giving their entire attention to the task, the pupils could set free the intuitive side of their personality. The aim was to generate something spontaneous in the moment, without judging it. Spolin was convinced that every type of acting could be learned and could be expressed creatively.

Among others, Spolin worked with actors from the improvisational theatre group The Compass Players, founded by her son Paul Sill, and from the improvisational theatre and comedy troupe The Second City, which was also co-founded by her son. There, she also furthered her acting theories and wrote her famous book "Improvisation for the Theater" (1963). Viola Spolin had a strong influence on the improv theatre movement in the USA, and is often referred to as the mother of today's improvisational theatre.

Paul Sills

Viola Spolin's son, Paul Sills, developed these methods further, and in 1955 founded the student theatre group **The Compass Players** in Chicago, the first professional improvisational theatre group as it is understood today.

In 1953 in Chicago, Paul Sills, Bernard Sahlins, and Howard Alk had founded the famous comedy and improvisational theatre group **The Second City**. The initial idea was to use Viola Spolin's techniques to develop forms of improvisational theatre for the stage. Today, comedy shows at The Second City are partially created through improvisation, and sometimes live before an audience. When the official part of the show ends, the audience is invited to stay to see the actors improvise and work on scenes for the next show. The audience's reaction decides which scenes are taken forward, and which are dropped.

The Second City is one of the most successful comedy and improvisational theatre stages. Famous actors and comedians such as Dan Ackroyd, Tina Fey, Mike Meyers, and Bill Murray first trod the boards there and started on their road to success.

Theatre of the Oppressed

Between 1950 and 1960, at the Núcleo do Teatro de Arena in São Paulo in Brazil, Augusto Boal developed the Theatre of the Oppressed. He aimed to create a theatre of the people and for the people, whose methods could help audiences stand up against oppression.

To this end, Boal invented a variety of forms, for example **Statue Theatre**, which involves representing conflicts of interest or situations of oppression by constructing statues out of people. The first representation is one's own image of reality (the real picture); one then moves on to representing one's ideal image, that is, what one hopes for (the ideal picture). Through this process, specific steps are identified to get from the real picture to the ideal picture.

Boal's best-known form of theatre is **Forum Theatre**, whereby the audience is usually also drawn into the performance. A difficult situation is introduced by the audience, and with the help of a joker the scene is played out, then discussed and modified by the audience. Then the characters – often weak, disadvantaged or oppressed people – are played on stage by the actors. The audience can replace actors and have them change the scene on stage. This allows solutions for difficult situations to be tried out and tested. Boal saw his methods as anti-authoritarian; it was not about finding the "right" solution, but to try out different ways and possibilities.

Keith Johnstone's Theatresports

Keith Johnstone taught at the Royal Court Theatre in London between 1956 and 1966, and called into question all the rules he himself had learned in school. His main criticism was that there was no room for creativity in schools. In his work as a teacher of acting, this led him to experiment with improvisation to bring more spontaneity and creativity to his actors. He emphasized collaboration and mutual support, since for him the group was the foundation of his work. He wanted actors to bring out the best ideas from their colleagues:

> But to block your partner's ideas is to be like the drowning man who drags down his rescuer.
>
> (Johnstone, 1981, p. 93)

Johnstone was also interested in the concept of status, and he discovered that scenes on stage seemed far more convincing if a clear difference in status between the actors could be perceived. He realized that each actor felt most comfortable with a certain status (high status = playing a hero; low status = playing the comedian), and that they would tend to settle into those roles. Through status exercises, Johnstone wanted to extend the actors' range of performance, and thus the variety of roles they could take on.

In 1971 Johnstone emigrated to Canada, and in 1977 founded The Loose Moose Theatre Company with Mel Tokken. Under Johnstone's leadership, Theatresports™ (Theatresports is an unregistered trademark) was developed, which to this day remains the most popular form of improvisational theatre.

Keith Johnstone developed Theatresports for three reasons:

1   He noticed that some actors lacked creativity and a passion for acting.
2   He found classical theatre to be too elitist, so he was trying for a more grass-roots and entertaining theatre for all.
3   He thought the separation of audience and actors was too inflexible, and he wanted the audience to have a greater influence.

As Johnstone had been a wrestling fan since he was a child, he had the idea of getting two teams to go head-to-head, from which the name Theatresports came about. Theatresports is a competition between improvisational theatre groups, with a referee and an MC to moderate the show through the evening and to get the audience warmed up. By making requests, or by active participation, the audience can play a large part in how the action on stage progresses. Johnstone wanted to generate a similar atmosphere as that found at sports events. By their applause, or by holding up coloured cards, the audience showed which team they had liked the best at the end of each round, with one team declared the winners at the end of the evening. Today, Theatresports is almost exclusively comedy, but Johnstone had originally intended it also to comprise serious and profound scenes. In 1979 he wrote his bestselling "Improvisation and Theatre" on the subject.

The year 1980 saw Theatresports spread to Europe, where it quickly became very popular. The first Theatresports World Championships took place in Germany in 2006. From the early years of the 21st century Theatresports and improvisational theatre spread around the globe, and countless forms and formats continue to emerge.

Del Close's Harold

American actor, writer, and acting coach Del Close, who also spent a long time in Chicago as a director at The Second City, created the first long form of improvisational theatre, known as the "Harold," which extends improvisation formats to fill an entire evening. He also co-wrote the well-known book "Truth in Comedy – the manual of improvisation" (1994).

Jonathan Fox's Playback Theater

Jonathan Fox invented Playback Theater in the United States around 1970. This is an interactive and improvised form of theatre, whereby a presenter asks a member of the audience to talk about a personal experience. This story is then "played back" by the actors on stage who do not attempt to run mechanically through the facts of the story; rather they try to get to its essence. The actors try to bring a deeper meaning to these everyday experiences, and thus facilitate new perspectives. A Playback evening covers several stories from audience members, which are all reproduced by the actors.

Playback theatre is also used in companies, for example at conferences, congresses, and celebrations. Staff members' stories are the focus, revealing things that have never been spoken about, and opening up new perspectives.

Ruth Zaporah's Action Theatre

The 1970s saw an explosion of experimentation with interdisciplinary performances in the San Francisco Bay Area. One form which emerged was "**Contact Improvisation**," a form of improvised dance whereby the movements were freshly created at any time, from the moment of contact.

At this time, performance artist Ruth Zaporah developed "Action Theatre," an improvised performance technique bringing together movements, dance, and speech. This is therefore a very corporeal form of improvisation. The focus is on perceiving the body, and being in the moment through the sensual experience of oneself and others. In 1995 she published her book on the subject: "Action Theatre: The Improvisation of Presence" (1995).

Improvisational theatre today

In today's improvisational theatre, the strands of the plot and the script are subject to free improvisation, meaning that every performance is both the premiere and the closing show, and will never be seen on the stage again. The players are given a theme by the audience and have to improvise around it. For example, the presenter may ask the audience to suggest a location where the next scene should take place, and this location then serves as a guideline or inspiration for the actors' scenes. These scenes will often also be accompanied by music improvised and played live, and since the players are creating freely on the spot, they are effectively the authors, directors, dramatic advisers, and actors all at the same time.

As at early 2018, the improvisational theatre website www.improwiki.com listed 1,128 improvisation groups worldwide, with the most in Germany (427), followed by the United States (136) and the United Kingdom (61). Despite its popularity with audiences, improvisational theatre is still not recognized as an art form in itself, and consequently receives very little subsidy from public funds. In the year 2000, Randy Dixon, a renowned improvisation actor and trainer in the USA, said that since improvisational theatre is oriented towards process rather than product, it will always struggle in a materialistic world where only the product tends to be accorded significance.

In recent years, many groups have continued to develop new forms of improvisational theatre. A brief overview of the best-known forms follows.

Short forms

These scenes usually only last a few minutes. There are hundreds of "games" in a variety of categories, such as games based on speech, or guessing. These are transferred to the stage in the form of an improvisation show.

Theatresports

In Theatresports the aforementioned games are used in the form of a contest. Two teams compete, and the audience decides the winner.

Long forms

Long forms last at least 15–20 minutes, and may even extend to fill an entire evening. The first long form, the Harold, was developed by Del Close. The actors are given a theme, and they spend the entire performance weaving together scenes and monologues relating to it. Autobiographical elements will often also be integrated. Many other long forms of improvisational theatre have now been developed, such as crime stories, whereby the players improvise a murder or a crime, and hunt for the perpetrator. The public can contribute, and help to discover leads and clues.

Music forms

Improvisational theatre often features music composed and played on the spot. Together with a musician, improvised operas or musicals may even be created. Such music may be in the form of short interludes during an improv show or Theatresports evening, or it may fill an entire evening by itself.

TV formats

Improvisational theatre has also made its mark in television. The show "Whose Line is it Anyway?", originally conceived as a comedy show for radio, was hugely successful, and was adapted for both British and American television. It also inspired "Frei Schnauze" from German broadcaster RTL.

Bibliography

Halpern, C., Close, D., and Johnson, H. K. (1994). *Truth in comedy – The manual of improvisation*. Colorado Springs: Meriwether.

Johnstone, K. (1981). *Improvisation and the theatre*. 2nd edn. London: Methuen Paperback.

Moreno, J. L. (1924). *Das Stegreiftheater*. Potsdam: des Vaters. Kiepenheuer.

Spolin, V. (1963). *Improvisation for the theater*. Chicago: Northwestern University Press.

Zaporah, R. (1995). *Action theatre: The improvisation of presence*. Berkeley: North Atlantic Books.

Online sources

Boyke, G. (2015). Improgruppen weltweit. *Improwiki*. Available at: https://improwiki.com/de/liste_improgruppen_weltweit [Accessed 12 July 2018].

Chapter 2

Applied improvisation

Introduction to applied improvisation

The term "applied sciences" refers to scientific disciplines that, along with their fundamental research element, can also usefully be applied in practical ways. From the early days of modern improvisational theatre, experiments were made into how to also apply its methods away from the stage. In the early 20th century, Jacob Levy Moreno developed psychodrama. Subsequently Brazil's Augusto Boal used improvisation in his support for oppressed people in his society, and Jonathan Fox deployed the form to help audience members with their personal experiences. Improvisational theatre's great potential for other target groups was clear from the start. Keith Johnstone began experimenting with its methods when he was a schoolteacher, and developed them later in his drama training sessions, addressing the question of how to bring improvisational theatre to non-actors and thereby foster creativity in them.

> Applied improvisation uses the principles, tools, practices, skills and mindsets developed in comedy, jazz and theatre and utilizes them for non-theatrical or performance purposes. Practitioners of applied improvisation facilitate workshops, for individuals or organisations, introducing them to these principles, tools etc. via solo, paired or group exercises, activities and games. Participants of applied improvisation workshops are able to integrate these principles; tools etc. into their daily lives. Personal development, team building, creativity, innovation and wellbeing are some of their areas that benefit from learning applied improvisation methods.
>
> (http://appliedimprovisation.network/about-applied-improvisation/, accessed 29 May 2018)

The basic principles of applied improvisation may be summarized in the following terms:

- attention and contact
- non-verbal communication
- co-creation

- spontaneity and intuition
- error culture and trust

In applied improvisation, these principles are no longer the exclusive preserve of actors on stage; rather they are applied to all other potential domains and professions. In this book, I concentrate on the application of improvisation techniques for coaches, trainers, and managers. Leadership, teamwork, creativity, storytelling, status, and presentation skills are all contemporary themes in professional training and management literature. They form an integral element of applied improvisation, which in turn offers a rich source of excellent methods to impart these skills.

The Applied Improvisation Network

It all began with a mailing list and a newsletter from Alain Rostain, who was one of the first to discover the value of improvisational theatre methods for companies. Upon his invitation, 30 pioneers met in San Francisco to exchange ideas on how they could implement elements of improvisational theatre in their own workplaces. In 2002, Paul Z. Jackson, Michael Rosenburg, and Alain Rostain founded the Applied Improvisation Network (AIN). Since then, this loose association has grown into a worldwide network (http://appliedimprovisation.network), whose members work together in joint projects and annual conferences to integrate applied improvisation methods into commerce, research, schools, therapy, and art. As of 2016, the network had 423 active members and 5,559 members in its Facebook group. Its annual conferences are attended by around 200 participants from around the world. Recent conferences were held in San Francisco (2012), Berlin (2013), Austin (2014), Montreal (2015), Oxford (2016), and Southern California (2017).

The aims of the network are as follows: (see http://
appliedimprovisation.network, accessed 29 May 2018)

- To promote the practice of applied improvisation
- To support members and practitioners of applied improvisation
- To develop methods of best practice
- To connect members to each other to foster collaborative working opportunities
- To partner with organizations to promote and teach applied improvisation to their members

Furthermore, AIN members hold the following convictions:
(see http://appliedimprovisation.network, accessed 29 May 2018)

- Improvisational practice has the power to improve the quality of human lives, communities, and organizational relationships.
- Play and spontaneity promote personal and professional growth and support innovation.

- Real collaboration is a valuable skill that helps organizational and group performance.
- Improvisation teaches generosity, cooperation, trust, and experimentation. This reduces anxiety, and releases creativity.
- These benefits are open to all people at any age, any walk of life, and especially to those who have never done it before!

In 2014, Barbara Tint and Adam Froerer compiled a Delphi study (a systematic, multi-step survey) for the Applied Improvisation Network, which summarized the 10 elements that AIN members considered most important to their work, as follows:

- Making your partner look good
- Yes . . . and
- Atmosphere of play
- Curious listening
- Complete acceptance
- Flexibility/spontaneity
- Focus on the here and now
- Risk taking
- Personal awareness/mindfulness
- Balance of freedom and structure

Many AIN members themselves work as trainers, consultants or coaches for companies. Some are teachers or psychotherapists; others work for environmental organizations, to cite just a few examples. However, they all work according to the basic principles of applied improvisation, and attempt to integrate these into their work. This movement has been very popular for a long time in the United States, where companies such as Facebook, Google, and Twitter use the methods to foster teamwork and co-creativity. In Europe, applied improvisation is only just becoming well-known, and here too is increasingly being implemented within companies.

Applied improvisation in further education

The methods of applied improvisation are also increasingly being integrated into further education, where they are particularly appropriate. Many company-internal and Master of Business Administration (MBA) programmes (above all in the United States) have been using its tools for a long time already, for example to help their staff and teams to better cope with change processes and complexity. These tools – of particular value in times of change – increase the effectiveness of managers by boosting their ability for spontaneous action and effective collaboration through work focused on the themes of presence, flexibility, and communicative competence. Indeed, managers and staff of organizations improvise all the time, even though they are not always aware of it.

There is often a "deficit-oriented" understanding of improvisation as being an ad hoc tactic to compensate for errors or fill in the gaps. However, purposeful training in the relevant elements of applied improvisation gives leaders in organizations and institutes new tools, allowing them to move away from merely reacting to change situations towards a creative approach. This work boosts the agile and adaptive qualities of leadership, along with a collaboration style that is more effective and more dynamically oriented towards the issues at hand.

In 2002 I began for the first time to incorporate methods and exercises from improvisational theatre into my workshops. Ever since then, in my seminars I have been using applied improvisation to address the following themes:

- presentation skills and techniques
- communication
- creativity and innovation
- status and leadership abilities
- storytelling
- teambuilding

In doing so, I have noticed that these methods appear somewhat risky to participants. Quite a few people think that "improvisation" means "acting" and that acting is something they are no good at. Simply uttering the words "role-play" in a group can straight away trigger some resistance. This is no surprise, as many people will already have had bad experiences with it in other types of training. Indeed, if the trainer fails to plan and implement these methods both professionally and carefully, it must be expected that they will run up against significant and justifiable resistance from participants.

This is why in my work I pay particular attention to the following:

Clarifying the assignment

I believe it is important for customers to know what they are in for, so I explain from the start that I intend to work with applied improvisation in the training, and I describe its advantages with regard to the customers' goals. In my proposition I then lay out how I will apply the appropriate elements of improvisational theatre. Customers should know what they are getting, and consciously decide to accept these methods.

Careful preparation

When planning seminars, I think very carefully about when and how I will implement various elements. The sequence of exercises should be logical. The start is particularly important, because – in keeping with Aristotle's assertion that the whole is greater than the sum of its parts – we can say that "the feast is in the first bite," so it should be as simple and as much fun as possible. After each exercise I make sure that the participants are clear about the aims of the exercise and what we are trying to learn from them. The exercises I use always have two goals: they should contribute to that learning process, and they should be fun.

Experiential learning cycle

In my seminars I work according to an experiential learning cycle, which assumes that learning only occurs through experience. The concept of the experiential learning cycle was developed by David Kolb (1984):

Concrete experience: a specific experience itself initiates learning.
Reflective observation: observations are made about the experience, and are reflected upon together.
Abstract conceptualization: generalizations are made about the experience and the principles behind it, giving rise to a theory together.
Active experimentation: the initial experience is revisited, and a new approach is applied, based on what has just been learned.

In my case, the experiential learning cycle follows the following pattern:

- improvisational theatre exercise or role-play
- observation and reflection
- constructing a theory together
- new exercises and role-plays

At the start, I usually run several exercises one after the other, without the reflection and conceptualization phases. Here it is important that the process flows, that the participants do not observe themselves during play, and above all that they do not start to be critical of themselves. At this stage, the flow is more important than doing it "right." Reflection and conceptualization only follow once this stage is finished. As the day moves on, I will start to introduce the reflection and conceptualization stages directly after each exercise, based on the experience the participants have just had.

Working as equals

Social competence is always central to my seminars, and I am certainly not the only expert on this in the room! All participants have an immeasurable wealth of experience and knowledge. I supply the methods so that the participants can learn even more about social competence, swap experiences, and learn from each other through mutual feedback, for example. As a setting for this work, I always place chairs in a circle, even though people are sometimes confused by the absence of the usual tables in the seminar room.

Clarity at the start

Participants should know what is in store for them, so I explain at the very beginning of the seminar that we will work with improvisational theatre, and what they can hope to gain from it. If I feel that people are unsure or resistant, we will talk about it at that point.

Fluid seminar planning

The course of events may be constantly changed as necessary, and adapted to the needs of the participants. I only suggest a rough sequence, with the approximate timings and themes of the day. That allows me to react flexibly to changes, to place the theme in the centre, and to improvise in order to maintain vitality in the group.

Working with volunteers

A typical feature of improvisational theatre is that volunteers are brought onto the stage *before* the exercise is described. This means that participants are taking a step into the unknown. This can decrease the pressure on them; precisely because they have not volunteered for a *specific* exercise, they are then relieved of the obligation to be particularly "good."

Improvising along with the participants

During many exercises, I improvise along with the participants. This further decreases the pressure on them, and prevents the impression that that I am somehow "opposite" them, especially when they see that their trainer is not above jumping into the unknown.

Failing with good humour

Failing with good humour is vital to improvisational theatre, and applies to participants and trainer alike. This is why I often start with exercises that allow people to develop the ability to fail with good humour. And if something does not work out for me, then I try to accept it with a smile; for example, in one seminar I was so overenthusiastic that I fell off my chair.

Figure 2.1 © Evi Fill

The participants' feedback was interesting, in that they found this harmless and unusual accident both amusing and instructive, precisely because I, as the trainer, was able to laugh at my own clumsiness.

Bibliography

Kolb, D. A. (1984). *Experiential learning – Experience as the source of learning and development*. Upper Saddle River: Prentice Hall.

Online sources

The Applied Improvisation Network. Available at: http://appliedimprovisation.network/about-applied-improvisation/ [Accessed 29 May 2018].
Tint, B. and Froerer, A. (2014). Delphi study summary. *Applied improvisation network*. Available at: http://appliedimprovisation.network/wp-content/uploads/2015/11/Delphi-Study-Summary.pdf [Accessed 29 May 2018].

Chapter 3

Foundations of improvisation

All forms of art involving improvisation, including theatre, dance, and music, share certain salient characteristics. We will now look at these, but only in relation to improvisational theatre. This chapter looks at three important foundations of improvisation:

1   Attention to the here and now
2   Accepting offers ("Yes, and...")
3   Making our partner look good

At the end of the chapter come the Ten Commandments of improvisation, a book of rules whose origins are unclear, but which has been central to the improvisation scene for a long time.

Attention to the here and now

Improvisation is not about planning ahead, but about giving our full attention to the "here and now." This principle of "here and now" is also very important in psychodrama, in Gestalt therapy and in group dynamics, and involves transferring all questions and problems from the scientific level (there and then) to the current interaction situation (here and now).

When applied to improvisational theatre, this means avoiding letting our thoughts stray from the matter at hand, and instead being entirely in the moment, as only this immediacy allows us to truly perceive ourselves and others. We can feel our own impulses, and be aware of where others are in the room and what they are doing. This is essential on stage.

When we are in the here and now, listening to other people is effortless, as we are already wrapped up in them. If we fail to listen to others properly, it is because we are "elsewhere" in our minds. For example, we may be thinking about how the other person is wrong, and how we are right, and we have already started preparing our counterargument. As soon as we start thinking ahead, we are already away from the present moment. Many people are delighted to remain fully focused on the here and now, even if it is only for a short while. One of the core skills that improvisational theatre methods can teach us is how to spend more of this hugely effective time in the here and now.

We have many exercises for this. Here are two:

Exercise

Walking through the Room

The players spread out evenly around the room. One player walks around within the room. As soon as she stops, another has to start.

Variant 2: As soon as another player starts to move, the walking player has to stop.

Exercise

Nod and Go

The players stand in a circle. One player begins; he must go to another and stand on that person's spot. However, he may not start until that player has nodded at him. As soon as that player has nodded to someone, and that person is walking towards him, he immediately has to look for a new position. But he, in turn, may only start moving once someone else has nodded to him, and so on. It is important to walk slowly. Ideally, everyone will always know who is currently searching for a new place, and will have their eyes on that person.

The "Yes, and . . ." principle

Another of improvisation's central rules is "accepting offers." An offer may be a phrase, a movement, or even a melody, and this rule requires accepting the offer with a "Yes," then reacting to it (and taking it further) with a subsequent "and."

By way of illustration, let's imagine the following situations on stage:

> Player A: *"Help! There's a bear!"*
> Player B: *"No, that's not a bear."*

Or:

> Player A: *"Mum, I'm sorry I came home late again."*
> Player B: *"I'm not your mum."*

Would you pay to see scenes like this? Probably not. Why do these scenes not draw us in? Because they feature blocking points that lead to a dead end! It would be difficult to develop these scenes further, and they will probably "die" before they have even get going.

In daily life we often hear "Yes, but . . .," because we do not wish to engage or agree with the other person, but we fear a "No" would sound impolite. With a "Yes, but . . .," the impulse moves forward briefly, but then immediately back again; it is generally a hidden block. (Psychologists have an in-joke: "'Yes, but . . .' – the shortest definition of neurosis.")

The renowned pioneer of applied improvisation, Kat Koppett, suggested 12 reasons for offers being blocked so often (Koppett, 2001, pp. 36–37):

1 Saying "yes" requires action.
2 Someone else might get more credit than we.
3 Someone we don't like is championing an idea.
4 Contradicting or debating is a way we have learned to feel smart.
5 The idea offered feels risky/silly/unoriginal.
6 There is a perceived or actual lack of resources.
7 We think the idea is "bad."
8 We think the idea is impossible to operationalize.
9 We like our own idea better.
10 We don't understand the idea.
11 We don't recognize that an offer has been made.
12 Conflict is exciting.

A "Yes" leads us into an uncertain future, whereas a "No" means no change, and thus appears to promise certainty. Keith Johnstone expressed it as follows (1981, p. 92):

> There are people who prefer to say "Yes," and there are people who prefer to say "No." Those who say "Yes" are rewarded by the adventures they have, and those who say "No" are rewarded by the safety they attain.

"Yes, and . . ." stands for the following:

Table 3.1 The meaning of Yes, and,…

YES	AND
Listening	Connecting
Acknowledging	Collaborating
Accepting	Building up
Encouraging	Creating

"Yes, and . . ." leads into an uncertain future

Accepting offers is the most important principle of improvisational theatre, as it is the only way we can formulate stories together on stage. But it does mean allowing ourselves to step into the unknown. This is precisely why it is so much easier to say "Yes, but . . ." or "No" – and so much more boring . . .

The "and" is, of course, essential. With this apparently unimportant little word we have not only accepted another's offer; we are now opening up a part of the story, and are creating something new together.

A scene with "Yes, and . . ." might look like this:

Player A: "*Help! There's a bear over there!*"
Player B: "*Yes, and it's coming over here!*"
Player A: "*Yes, and we'll have to fight it.*"
Player B: "*Yes, and I've got my Thermos flask with me.*"
Player A: "*Yes, and there's some very strong schnapps in it.*"
Player B: "*Yes, and we can get the bear drunk with it.*"

Figure 3.1 © Evi Fill

If both players work well together and build off each other, the result is a story that, even for the players themselves, is surprising, new, amusing, inspiring, and so on.

"Yes, and . . ." can also be an attitude

Of course, the "Yes, and . . ." need not always be explicitly stated or said out loud; rather, it should ideally be understood as an attitude within a person. On stage, we can also say "Yes, and . . ." to an offer by saying "No," as in the following scene:

Player A: "*It really annoys me that you never take the trash out!*"
Player B: "*No, you're wrong there; you're the one who never does anything around the house!*"

The offer by Player A is in fact an incitement to fight, and Player B accepts the offer to fight and builds upon it, even though she starts her phrase with "No."

"Yes, and . . ." in training

Once we have all met each other and warmed up a little, I introduce the idea of accepting offers, as it is the precondition for any further work with improvisational theatre methods. The "Yes, and . . ." will frequently create a very positive atmosphere among the participants.

I bring the theme into my seminars with the following exercises:

Exercise

No – yes, but . . . – yes, and . . .

This exercise is done in pairs, in three rounds. I demonstrate each round with a partner.

First round:

One player makes an offer to another, who must answer with a "No," then make their own offer:

Player A: "*Let's go skiing today.*"
Player B: "*No, I don't feel like it. Let's go to the cinema.*"
Player A: "*No, I haven't got any money; let's go to the park instead.*"
. . . and so on.

Second round:

One player makes the other an offer, who must answer with a "Yes, but . . .," then again make their own offer:

> Player A: *"Let's go out to eat today."*
> Player B: *"Yes, but I'm on a diet. But we could go for a run."*
> Player A: *"Yes, but my knee hurts. Let's go to a party instead."*
> . . . and so on.

Third round:

One player makes an offer, and the other must answer with a "Yes, and . . .," which will then lead to a further offer:

> Player A: *"Let's found a company today."*
> Player B: *"Yes, and we can sell chickens."*
> Player A: *"Yes, and they can sing."*
> Player B: *"Yes, and our chickens sell like hot cakes."*
> Player A: *"Yes, and we can retire on all the money."*
> . . . and so on.

After each three rounds I ask the pairs how each round had felt, and what the differences were between the "No," the "Yes, but . . ." and the "Yes, and . . .." I often then hear that the "Yes, but . . ." is a "No" in disguise, and that the third round with the "Yes, and . . ." was the round that developed best, and enabled both participants to generate a story together.

Exercise

First do Accept Loses

Two players come on stage. They have to block any offer the other makes. If a player accepts an offer, she will be replaced.

Participants usually greatly enjoy being allowed to block. At the same time, this exercise increases their awareness of what a block actually is, and why blocks lead to a dead end.

Exercise

First do Block Loses

Two players come on stage. They have to accept any offer the other makes. If a player blocks an offer, he will be replaced. This exercise lets participants learn about recognizing and accepting offers.

Making our partner look good

Another important basis for any type of improvisation is that it always involves interaction with other people, for example the audience. This interaction can only be effective when all other players are comfortable in the situation. This means that we have to truly engage with each other, listen to each other, accept each other's offers, and generally strive to make each other "look good," so that everyone can show their best sides. This behaviour is unfamiliar to many: instead of my "I," your "You" takes priority, and on top of that, I'm even expected to be helpful to you! Repressing your own narcissism even temporarily can be rewarded by a better and more effective scene. For example, if a player makes a mistake, then we should run to their aid, and support them:

> Player A is setting up skis and snowboards. She is obviously working in a sports equipment shop.
> Player B does not grasp this, enters the shop and says, *"Hello, I'd like a Frankfurter."*
> Player A: *"Ah, do please come in! Today we are inaugurating our new shop – the buffet is over here."*
> Player A recognizes that Player B has not acknowledged or understood her offer, so she brings the two ideas together herself.

If the players had not supported each other, the scene may have looked like this:

> Player B: *"Hello, I'd like to buy a television."*
> Player A: *"Can't you see this is a sports equipment shop?"*

Of course we can also continue with this scene, but the beginning is already pretty destructive. Many find it difficult to concentrate on other people and on collaborating with them, rather than concentrating on themselves. But in improvisation, as in every other form of teamwork, it is essential to do so, because of the synergy that is born from it. This weaving together of strengths that further reinforce each other has tremendous power, and will delight players and spectators alike.

We can practise this skill in almost any exercise. The more inexperienced participants are at improvising, the more they tend to focus on themselves. This means they must be dragged out of their self-reflection (and often also self-criticism), and helped to bring their entire attention to the here and now. This is easiest to achieve if we concentrate on the other players, such as in the following exercise:

Exercise

Complimenting Each Other

Two players approach each other and make complimentary comments about the other. These should reflect genuine sentiments, so we need to look carefully for what we genuinely like and appreciate about the other.

The more experience people have with improvisation, the better they are able not only to concentrate on others, but also to spot when others need help. Talented improvisation actors are able to act alongside beginners on stage and still create interesting scenes and stories. Indeed, there is also an improvisation format that involves bringing a member of the audience on stage, and for the entire show that person will play with the expert improvisation actor.

Ten Commandments of Improvisation

A variety of improvisation rules are used throughout the discipline, and many can be found on the Internet. The actor, author, and teacher Del Close simply has this to say about it: "The only rule is that there are no rules."

Here I would like to introduce the "Ten Commandments of Improvisation" that are the best-known, and are commonly found throughout the world of improvisational theatre. Unfortunately, I was unable to find out who first wrote them down, but they are vital not only for improvisation, but for every kind of creative teamwork.

1 **Thou shalt not block.**
   As described earlier, this rule concerns accepting offers from others.
2 **Thou shalt always retain focus.**
   On stage and in all collaborative work, it is vital to maintain focus; that is, to know what to pay attention to. This may be other people, or indeed ideas.

3   **Thou shalt not shine above thy teammates.**
   This rule tells us not to unnecessarily make ourselves the centre of attention
   or leave too little space for our colleagues.

4   **To gag is to commit a sin that will be paid for.**
   Many believe that improvisational theatre is about telling jokes and trying to be
   funny. A gag will get a laugh for a moment or two, but always to the detriment
   of the story and the whole process. This rule may also usefully be applied to
   other types of collaboration, where jokes are often at the cost of other people.

5   **Thou shalt always be changed by what is said to you.**
   This rule is about letting ourselves be influenced and changed by others, as
   this is the only way to create anything new together at all.

6   **Thou shalt not waffle.**
   This rule speaks for itself, both on stage and in daily life.

7   **When in doubt, break the routine.**
   In the context of the stage, this means breaking with routine when we feel the
   action may be getting boring. In the context of teamwork, it may mean trying
   out new things when we are stuck in a rut.

8   **To wimp is to show thy true self.**
   Whoever hides behind others and lacks the courage to show himself will
   often hinder successful teamwork, both on stage and in the workplace.

9   **S/he that tries to be clever, is not; while s/he that is clever, doesn't try.**
   The less we strive to be creative or original, the more creative and original we are.

10 **When thy faith is low, thy spirit weak, thy good fortune strained, and thy
   team losing, be comforted and smile, because it just doesn't matter.**
   Of course, this is easier said (and done) on stage than in real life, but the fact
   remains that many problems will seem far less significant 10 years from now!

Exercises to lead into improvisation

Attention to the here and now

1   **Ball Circle**
   Procedure: All players stand in a circle. They throw a ball to each other in a
      fixed sequence. Next, several more balls are introduced, which must also
      be thrown in the same sequence. Finally the players break their circular
      formation and move freely around the room, while still throwing the balls
      to each other in the same sequence.
   Themes:
      Attention to the here and now: The moment anybody loses their focus,
         the ball will fall to the floor.

2   **Delayed Replies**
   Procedure: All players stand in a circle. One comes into the centre. The first
      player asks her a simple question (e.g. What is your shoe size? Where did
      you last go on holiday?). The player in the middle does not answer yet,

but turns to the second player, who then asks her a similar question. She still does not answer, turning instead to a third player. When that player asks their question, the player in the middle answers the first question. The sequence continues in this way.

Here is an example:

Player A: "*Where did you last go on holiday?*" Player in the middle says nothing.
Player B: "*Where do you live?*" Player in the middle says nothing.
Player C: "*What is your shoe size?*" Player in the middle: "*Italy.*"
Player D: "*What colour are your eyes?*" Player in the middle: "*Zurich.*"
Player E: "*What's your favourite food?*" Player in the middle: "*42.*"
. . . and so on.

Themes:

Attention to the here and now: Although the player in the middle has to keep her answers in her head, she must also be in the here and now if she is not to miss subsequent questions.

Contact and getting to know each other: The questions and answers allow players to get to know each other better (although the questions should not be too personal, to avoid embarrassment).

It is fun to fail: Only a very few can manage more than a few questions, and this doesn't matter anyway.

3   **Nod and Go**

Procedure: The players stand in a circle. One player begins; he must go to another and stand on that person's spot. However, he may not start until that player has nodded at him. As soon as that player has nodded to someone, and that person is walking towards him, he immediately has to look for a new position. But he, in turn, may only start moving once someone else has nodded to him, and so on. It is important to walk slowly. Ideally, everyone will always know who is currently searching for a new place, and will have their eyes on that person.

Themes:

Attention to the here and now: As soon as a player stops paying attention, they will no longer know who is looking for a new position.

Making our partner look good: We must give everything to the game, rather than our own needs, as we must nod.

4   **Walking and Standing at the Same Time**

Procedure: Everyone walks around the room, trying to stand still and at the same time walk off again.

Themes:

> **Attention to the here and now**: Every player must concentrate entirely on the others for this to work at all.

5   **Walking through the Room**

Procedure: The players spread out evenly around the room. One player walks around within the room. As soon as she stops, another has to start.

Variant 2: As soon as another player starts to move, the walking player has to stop.

Themes:

> **Attention to the here and now**: It is immediately clear if anybody is at all inattentive, as there will be pauses, and the game will not be able to flow.

Accepting offers – Yes, and . . .!

1   **First to Accept Loses**

Procedure: Two players come on stage. They have to accept any offer the other makes. If a player blocks an offer, he will be replaced.

Themes:

> **Accepting offers**: The players see how difficult it can be to truly accept all offers and to genuinely remain open to others and their ideas.

2   **First to Block Loses**

Procedure: Two players come on stage. They have to block any offer the other makes. If a player accepts an offer, she will be replaced.

Themes:

> **Accepting offers**: The players see that stories cannot develop if offers are constantly blocked.

3   **Freeze Tag**

Procedure: All players stand in a line. Two players come forward and start to improvise a scene freely. Once it becomes more or less clear what the scene is about, the last player in the line calls "Freeze," at which point the players stop, and freeze in position. The next player in the line comes forward, taps one of the players on the shoulder and copies their body pose as closely as possible. The original player then goes back to the line.

Then the two players begin a completely new scene, except that their first offer is the body pose taken from the previous scene. This works well if a totally new scene can be created on the basis of that same body pose. For example, in the first scene the player was picking apples from a tree, and the new player is changing a lightbulb.

Themes:

> **Accepting offers**: The players learn that even a body pose can represent an offer.

> **Teamwork**: Interesting scenes only arise if both players cooperate and open up to each other.

4   Hollywood Swing

Procedure: This exercise involves two players. One is a cinema director who has just made a film, and the other is somebody who has seen the film. For example:

Player A: *"You made a great film! All about ants!"* (The subject does not matter.)

From now on, all answers must begin with, *"Yes, exactly, and . . .."*

Player B: *"Yes, exactly, and the ants climb up all the buildings."*

Player A: *"Yes, exactly, and they eat their way through the walls."*

Player B: *"Yes, exactly, and the humans have to flee from the ants."*

. . . and so on.

Thus, the players draft out a film together, and neither knew in advance where it would lead. The important thing to talk about is not the "making of," but the plot of the film.

Themes:

Accepting offers: The players develop a film story together and recognize how much fun it can be when every idea is picked up and taken further.

5   No – Yes, but . . . – Yes, and . . .

Procedure: This exercise is done in pairs, in three rounds.

First round:

One player makes an offer to another, who must answer with a "No," then make their own offer:

Player A: *"Let's go skiing today."*

Player B: *"No, I don't feel like it. Let's go to the cinema."*

Player A: *"No, I haven't got any money; let's go to the park instead."*

. . . and so on.

Second round:

One player makes the other an offer, who must answer with a "Yes, but . . .," then again make their own offer:

Player A: *"Let's go out to eat today."*

Player B: *"Yes, but I'm on a diet. But we could go for a run."*

Player A: *"Yes, but my knee hurts. Let's go to a party instead."*

. . . and so on.

Third round:

One player makes an offer, and the other must answer with a "Yes, and . . .,"
which will then lead to a further offer:

Player A: "*Let's found a company today.*"
Player B: "*Yes, and we can sell singing chickens.*"
Player A: "*Yes, and our chickens sell like hot cakes.*"
Player B: "*Yes, and we can retire on all the money.*"
. . . and so on.

After each three rounds I ask the pairs how each round had felt, and what the
differences were between the "No," the "Yes, but . . ." and the "Yes, and
. . . ."

Themes:

Accepting offers: The players learn the power of "Yes, and . . .," and
discover how these two simple words can really help a story develop.

6   **Today's Tuesday!**

Procedure: Player A makes a blind offer, as follows:

Player A: "*Today's Tuesday!*"

This is termed a blind offer because Player A does not know himself where
he wants to take it.

Player B then accepts the offer, but with great emotion. It does not matter if
this is sad, happy, angry etc., but he must not think about it in advance. If
the sentiment is strong, the player explains why. For example:

Player A says: "*Today's Tuesday!*"
Player B becomes sadder and sadder, and then says: "*It was on a Tuesday
this time last year that my mother died.*"

Only now do both players know what the blind offer means, and they
can play on.

Themes:

Accepting offers: The players learn about blind offers.

Emotions: The players learn that strong emotions make for an exciting
scene, and can bring about change.

Making our partner look good

1   **Blind Offer**

Procedure: All players stand in a circle. One player goes into the centre and assumes an abstract pose. Another player joins him, and extends his pose with one of his own, making a larger static picture.

For example, Player A kneels down and Player B comes and gives him an imaginary communion wafer.

Themes:

Making our partner look good: The second player gives meaning to the position the first player has assumed.

Accepting offers: The players learn that striking a pose can also represent an offer.

2   **Complimenting Each Other**

Procedure: Two players take turns to compliment each other. These comments should be genuine.

Themes:

Making our partner look good: The players have to really engage with each other to come up with genuine compliments and to make each other look good.

Bibliography

Johnstone, K. (1981). *Improvisation and the theatre*. 2nd edn. London: Methuen Paperback.
Koppett, K. (2001). *Training to imagine – Practical improvisational theatre techniques to enhance creativity, teamwork, leadership and learning*. Sterling: Stylus.

Chapter 4

Teamwork

Working groups versus teamwork

Working in groups is a relatively old form of collaboration. Our distant ancestors almost certainly had to work in groups when hunting, an activity as dangerous as it is unpredictable.

Figure 4.1 © Evi Fill

Teams, if they are "real" teams, are a much younger "invention." Even so, they already appear to be a fixed feature of modern organizations. Furthermore, many companies see teamwork as a kind of "magic bullet" to increase productivity and the quality of work. However, the results frequently fail to meet expectations. The resulting frustration can be so widespread as to give teamwork a poor reputation, usually accompanied by calls for a return to traditional leadership with clear instructions. But neither overblown expectations nor criticism of group/teamwork are rewarding attitudes. A more promising approach is to consider the following questions: What is a working group, and what is a true team? When do we need groups, and when should we deploy teams?

Let's be clear from the start: not every form of working together is teamwork! Five employees packing promotional material for a customer offer are not working as a team. Even if they have to discuss how to do it, it is still not teamwork; they are simply working together. In fact, very few groups work as teams – even if they are convinced they do. They "merely" cooperate, meaning that a single leader or manager can initiate, control, correct as necessary, and thus "centrally" direct an assignment.

True teams look very different, and ideally they should only be deployed to solve the most difficult issues. These are complex tasks and problems of the business that are beyond the experience of any individual – for example, the managers – and that require the expertise and input of an array of people. Teamwork is meaningful and necessary when answers are needed that are truly useful, and that have not already been found in the past. Little is more frustrating to teams than to pour their efforts into an "essential" activity, only to find that a quick look at the specialist literature, or some advice from the appropriate expert would have sufficed. Such situations lead many people to steer clear of so-called "teamwork."

However, when the problem at hand really does require new approaches – and thus innovation, creativity, and being able to handle complexity or uncertainty – then it is time to bring a team in. A good example is the difference between classical theatre and improvisational theatre. In classical theatre, a director decides how the scenes will play out, whereas improvisational theatre as an artistic process is interactive, brought about and directed by all concerned. A similar comparison may be made of a classical orchestra and a jazz band.

Figure 4.2 © Evi Fill

Figure 4.3 © Evi Fill

The principal difference between a team and a group is that the members of a team influence each other's work, and allow others to influence them. They inspire, correct, contradict, and encourage each other. To enable this, it is also important that they have diverse knowledge and backgrounds, so that the team-work can be genuinely fruitful due to their being more likely to bounce varied ideas off each other.

However, this does not mean that groups and teams are somehow at odds. Groups in the sense of centrally directed working groups do have their strengths. Let us imagine we are sitting in a theatre, when a fire breaks out. Which rescue team would we prefer to see? A creative group of talented firefighters from a variety of backgrounds, who set about working together to develop the best rescue strategy? Or a well-practised group of professionals under the leader-ship of an experienced crew chief who gives clear orders. The main point of this question is that carrying out routine tasks, standardized procedures and established processes does not require "real" teams. It goes without saying, however, that fire brigades do also need "real" teamwork when they are faced with unpredictable and unfamiliar situations, and must work together to find original solutions for them.

The ideal is to successfully combine both ways of working so that they can reinforce each other through their differing characteristics. We might sum this up by saying that centrally controlled working groups deliver faster results, and real teams deliver more effective results; and we can already see from this that neither is "better" or "worse." It all depends on the goals and the circumstances. From a technical and creative point of view, team decisions and team output may lead to higher quality and higher levels of acceptance among stakeholders than the results of working groups would. A successful team delivers more than could be achieved by the sum of the individual efforts of its members. However, true teamwork is not without its disadvantages: teamwork naturally requires far more communication, and takes longer. Furthermore, leading teams is much harder! In a working group the boss sets the goals, and coordinates and controls the work, whereas in a team all participants (including the boss!) may take the lead and/or allow themselves to be led.

To sum up: for routine tasks or those requiring rapid planning and decisions, centrally led working groups are the most appropriate approach. But when a situ-ation is highly complex and requires the creative abilities of each individual, then teamwork is required.

Openness and trust in teamwork

Companies are held to be rationally directed organizations, and rational plans and goals are certainly also necessary to them. But in fact this would only seem to be half of the story: decisions and processes in companies do not depend solely on carefully thought-through plans and solid concepts. What we often cannot see from "outside" is just how much irrationality can run through an organization, and to what extent any company may be shaped by the emotional and irrational behaviours of its staff. Managers and staff used to be expected to concentrate on the "job at hand," but for a long time now "interpersonal skills" have also been expected. Rarely does a job ad appear without terms such as "team player," "social skills," and so on.

To get to the bottom of this phenomenon, Google looked closely at the elements that make up successful teams (Duhigg, 2016). It turned out that gathering the sharpest minds together was not that important! A far more significant element was a concept that the author named "psychological safety." This describes the extent to which team members feel safe in the team; that is, how openly they are able to speak (e.g. about conflicts in the team, but also about private problems), and how much faith they have in other team members. It is also important that all team members have an equal opportunity to speak, rather than certain team members speaking more than others.

In this context, the term "**psychological safety**" originates with Amy Edmondson (2013). In teams with psychological safety, everyone can speak their mind, questions may be asked, mistakes may be spoken about without punishment, and doubts may be expressed at the right time. There must also be confidence that contradicting views, diversity, differences, problems, and conflicts may be brought to the table rather than being allowed to fester, only to emerge later in dummy conflicts at the practical level. "Psychological safety" ensures that all team members feel at home in the team, and that new and creative ideas can be examined and adopted.

But how do we generate this psychological safety in a team, and how do we support the team skills of its members? Still today, "real" teamwork remains little more than a marginal theme in most manager training, and it cannot be learned from books. This is because we cannot really think our way into social competence; rather, we must gain it through experience. Methods from improvisational theatre allow us to develop personal and social competencies in a practical and vibrant way, and achieve that elusive "psychological safety" in our teams.

Applied improvisation for teamwork

Improvisational theatre is per se teamwork.

> The only star in Improv is the ensemble itself.
>
> (Halpern et al., 1994, p. 37)

This is true even if a player is alone on stage, as she has to work with the audience. Interesting scenes and stories may only be created on stage when the players commit to interacting with each other, influencing each other, and inspiring each other. There is no director giving instructions from the wings, so the quality of the stories arises directly from the quality of the collaboration. Much of the training for improvisational theatre actors is concerned with practising this collaboration.

However, improvisational theatre does have its limits. For example, if there are open conflicts or significant friction in teams, then other methods of team development need to be "activated." One option is Augusto Boal's Forum Theatre. This special method of improvisation allows conflicts to be replayed, and new solutions to be sought and immediately tested. This may involve actors playing the roles, or the staff members themselves.

Using methods from improvisational theatre is particularly useful in teams in situations such as the following:

* A team is being re-constructed, and needs to be up and running.
* An existing team wishes to invest in its efficiency and collaborative atmosphere.
* A team wishes to fully exploit its creative and innovative potential, and is looking for the tools to be able to do so.

The most important foundations of successful collaboration, which can very effectively be trained using methods from improvisational theatre, are as follows:

* Openness and trust
* Listening and maintaining focus
* Accepting and developing offers ("Yes, and...")
* Taking the lead, and allowing ourselves to be led

Nurturing openness and trust in teams

Without a doubt, trust is a crucial source of security in daily business. To create a climate of trust, openness must exist or be created. In practice, this means that we must pluck up our courage and speak in personal terms about how we feel about a situation. This process was described in the "Johari Window" model by Joseph Luft and Harry Ingham (Luft, 1963), a frequently overlooked classic of management literature.

Table 4.1 The Johari Window (From Luft, 1963, p. 22 by courtesy of Dr Rachel E. Luft)

	Known to self	Not known to self
Known to others	Open or Arena	Blind Spot
Not known to others	Hidden or Façade	Unknown

The aim of this model is to expand a group's "room for manoeuvre"; that is, the space for free activity, where the "real" teamwork takes place. This is possible as follows:

The "Hidden or Façade" area can be made to shrink if individuals share personal information that has a bearing on the situation. This increases the overall room for manoeuvre.

The "Blind Spot" area shrinks when we receive feedback from others in the group, teaching us new things about ourselves, and allowing us to balance out our image of ourselves against how others see us. This also increases the overall room for manoeuvre.

The "Unknown" area can also be shrunk; however, this is better done through psychotherapy, and is scarcely possible or meaningful in a seminar or training session.

When the "Open or Arena" area of free activity expands, members of the group are free to be and act according to their nature, and can also relate to the others as they "really" are. In such an atmosphere of mutual trust, there is less need to hide feelings or thoughts that are relevant to the situation.

The Johari Window model clearly shows that one criterion for successful teamwork is the expansion of the area of free activity. The key foundations for any collaboration are openness and trust, which can only arise through processes that boost self-confidence and our courage to be open. The underlying construct we are striving for may ultimately be described as a "feeling of safety" in our dealings with the world.

One exercise that is suitable for the start of training a team, and which strengthens openness and trust in the team, is as follows:

Exercise

What I would have liked to be!

One player comes to the front and introduces himself before the group. In doing so, he should think about what he would have liked to have done in his life. Everything is possible; for example, he may have wanted to be the first human on Mars, an organic farmer with five kids, and so on. He introduces himself and relates all the details about his imaginary "other life," both professional and private. The themes should not be arbitrary; rather they should genuinely reflect a long-standing wish, a talent, an interest, etc. He should "pay homage" to these desires as he brings them on stage.

This exercise is particularly interesting if the group members already know each other well, as it will reveal previously hidden sides of other colleagues. Furthermore, opening up about themes like this generates even more trust.

Listening and maintaining focus

In improvisational theatre, when we talk about maintaining focus, this means acknowledging who should be the central point of the scene we are working on. A decision is made on the spot as to who is suppressing their own impulses in order to listen and open up. This focus leads almost "automatically" to a more regular sharing out of "speaking time." This important element of interesting scenes – and thus a desired effect on the improvisation stage – can just as usefully be applied to collaboration in the office.

To this end, a good exercise for teams is "Spider's Web":

Exercise

Spider's web

All players stand in a circle, and imaginary webs will be strung out corresponding to words belonging to categories, such as countries, dishes, flowers, cars, and so on.

For example, in the first web, Player A says to Player D "*Italy*"; Player D says to Player B "*Portugal*," and so on until every player has taken a turn. This web is then repeated in exactly the same order. Next, a second web is spun with another category, with new words being called out, in a different order. Then a third web is created using words from a third category, again in a different order. Finally, an attempt is made to get the participants to call out all three webs simultaneously by having them throw balls to each other in the same sequences as the three different webs.

When "webs" such as these fall apart, it is usually due to the following:

• A player is not paying attention, and not listening to the others.
• A player is not making an effort to maintain contact with the players passing words to her.

- A player is not making sure that her words are being properly received by the other players (e.g. she is mumbling, speaking in the wrong direction, or speaking too quietly).

This exercise gets right down to the principles of effective communication in teams. Just as in "real" life, information can easily be lost. With this exercise we can clearly recognize problems in team communication, we can make out patterns, and we can already start to address the weaknesses.

Another exercise, called "Counting to 21," is carried out by many improvisation groups and troupes of actors before the actors go on stage. This exercise shows to what extent the group is ready to work together.

Exercise

Counting to 21

The group stands in a circle, and counts to 21. Each individual calls out numbers, but there is no fixed sequence of players, and whenever two individuals call out a number at the same time, the count must begin again from zero.

This exercise is not about working out tricks, but about being fully focused on the teamwork and being in the here and now. The exercise shows very quickly how well the members of the team work together. Several rounds may be necessary, or indeed the exercise may not work out at all. Some teams, however, manage to get to 21 at the first attempt, and can even go on to count all the way to a hundred. Whatever the result, it can bring about valuable reflection on how the team works.

Next comes an exercise that is particularly useful to practise listening: "Swapping Stories."

Exercise

Swapping stories

The players form pairs, and tell each other a short personal story. They then swap pairs and repeat to their new partner the story they have just heard, telling the story as if it had happened to themselves, and using as many of the same words, gestures, and feelings as possible. This is repeated for several more rounds. Then all players stand in a circle, and each relates the last story they heard.

This exercise helps us learn to pay attention not only to the content but also to the body language and the feelings behind the story.

The "Yes, and . . ." principle in teams

Trust requires generosity: a "competitive" atmosphere – where ideas are shut down, and where each person attempts to block the other or seeks to raise their profile at the cost of the others – is enemy number one for successful teamwork. Trust can be created when people are free to assume that their ideas and opinions will be given a ready ear, will be taken seriously, and that others may pick up the ideas so that innovation may occur.

Improvisational theatre offers exercises that are very suitable for highlighting this quality of collaboration in a team, for example "One-Word Stories."

Exercise

Word at a time story

All participants sit in a circle and attempt to tell a meaningful story, with each individual adding just one word at a time.

Here are two examples of how such a story may pan out; in the story to the left, offers are blocked, whereas on the right, offers are accepted:

Table 4.2 Two Examples for Word at a time stories

Offers blocked	Offers accepted
Player A: "Stefan"	Player A: "Stefan"
Player B: "*is*"	Player B: "*is*"
Player C: **"*not*"**	Player C: "*a*"
Player D: "*called*"	Player D: "*Casanova.*"
Player E: "*Stefan.*"	Player E: "*He*"
Player F: "*He's*"	Player D: "*goes*"
Player G: "*off*"	Player E: "*to*"
Player H: "*to*"	Player F: "*the*"
Player I: "*the*"	Player G: "*pub*"
Player J: "*pub*"	Player H: "*where*"
Player K: **"*but*"**	Player I: "*he*"
Player L: **"*turns*"**	Player J: "*meets*"
Player M: "*back*"	Player K: "*a*"
Player N: "*home.*"	Player L: "*beautiful*"
. . . and so on.	Player M: "*woman.*"
	. . . and so on.
Players C, K, and L block the preceding players' offers.	This story works better because each player attempts to build on the previous player's input.

Yet another exercise requiring that offers be accepted, and which again shows how well a team works together, is called "What Comes Next?"

Exercise

What comes next?

Two players stand on stage, and one begins with the words "*What comes next?*" Members of the audience then tell him what he should do or say. He follows the suggestions, then says "*What comes next?*" for the other player, and so on. The players only do or say what the audience members suggest, never blocking the offers.

Most scenes begin something like this:

Player A: "*What comes next?*"
Audience: "*Go over to the other and hold out your hand.*" – Player A does this.
Player B: "*What comes next?*"
Audience: "*Turn around.*" – Player B does this.
. . . and so on.

In many teams almost every offer will be blocked at first. The audience needs to gradually get the idea that they should be accepting each other's offers, in order to create any kind of meaningful story:

Player A: "*What comes next?*"
Audience: "*Go over to the other and hold out your hand.*"
Player B: "*What comes next?*"
Audience: "*You say, 'Oh! It's the boss!'*"
Player B: "*Oh! It's the boss!*"
Player A: "*What comes next?*"
Audience: "*You run your fingers through your hair nervously and say, 'Ah, our department head, Huber!'*"
Player A: "*Ah, our department head, Huber!*"
Player B: "*What comes next?*"
Audience: "*You say, 'I'm quite surprised to see you in a place like this!'*"
Player B: "*I'm quite surprised to see you in a place like this!*"
. . . and so on.

Figure 4.4 © Evi Fill

Table 4.3 An example for a word at a time story

Difficulty taking the lead	Taking the lead
Player A: "*I*"	Player A: "*I*"
Player B: "*prefer*"	Player B: "*go*"
Player C: "*to*"	Player C: "*to*"
Player D: "*go*"	Player D: "*work.*"
Player E: "*further*"	Player E: "*Companies*"
Player F: "*back.*"	Player F: "*generate*"
Player E: "*There*"	Player G: "*money.*"
Player F: "*it's*"	Player H: "*Money*"
Player G: "*nice*"	Player I: "*destroys*"
Player H: "*and*"	Player J: "*people's*"
Player I: "*comfy*"	Player K: "*lives.*"
Player K: "*for*"	
Player I: "*me.*"	
This is a typical story whereby none of the players wishes to take on responsibility.	This is how a story can look if nobody wishes to give up the lead. None of the players is using linking words or adjectives to flesh out the story; each just tries to push the story forward in the direction they want to go.

Taking the lead and allowing ourselves to be led

As discussed earlier, in real teamwork, not only will the managers lead; rather, all participants will take the lead equally. Such collaboration is characterized by the perfect balance of input from all team members. This means that every team member must be capable of taking the lead, and also surrendering the lead again.

The "Word at a Time Story" can demonstrate who in a team is taking the lead too much, and who has difficulty doing so.

A good story (and good teamwork) needs both of the elements of leading and being led. Is it my job to push the content of the story forward, for example with nouns and verbs? Or is it my job to tie the plot together with linking words or adjectives? The story remains at the centre and each team member should monitor their own needs and desires, and set them aside if necessary for the sake of the story's development. This is mirrored in genuine teamwork, where the task of the group should remain at the centre, perhaps at the cost of individuals' different agendas and interests.

Psychological safety

An important issue in every team is to what extent the team members are prepared to lay themselves open, and in which areas:

- I'm not sure what I'm doing: questions, lack of expertise, etc.
- I don't agree: criticism, conflicts, objections, mistakes, etc.
- I have an idea: suggestions, ideas, creativity, etc.

The more team members are prepared to confess a lack of expertise, to question accepted notions, to speak openly about conflicts, to point out mistakes, and to put forward their own ideas, the higher the level of psychological safety within the team will be. And only then can the various experiences and expertise of the team members come into play, allowing the diversity within the team to truly unfold!

By deploying methods from improvisational theatre we can support the vital element of psychological safety. It is of course vital that the trainer, the layout of the workshop, and the setting themselves all contribute to this feeling of safety.

Methods from improvisational theatre

We see new sides of ourselves and others.
In improvisational theatre we are constantly slipping into new roles. By doing so we are not only extending our repertoire, but also learning about sides of ourselves we are unfamiliar with. The team will be more closely bonded when we discover new things about the others.

We try new things and make ourselves vulnerable.
In every workshop deploying these methods we are trying new things. For example, we may volunteer to participate, without actually knowing what we are letting ourselves in for. We are thus making ourselves vulnerable in front of the others and taking a risk. This boosts mutual trust.

We make mistakes and – hopefully – laugh about them.
Naturally we will sometimes fall on our faces. Hopefully we can laugh about this and thus build up a tolerance to mistakes within the team.

We have experiences together, which binds us more strongly.
When we work with methods from improvisational theatre, only a very small proportion of the training session is taken up with the trainer talking, or with discussions. Most of the time is spent improvising with each other, that is, experiencing something together. Participants will often be able to remember scenes for a long time, and will still be talking about them years later. These joint experiences as a team strengthen the feeling of belonging together.

We have fun and laugh together.
Many exercises and games are quite simply fun. Laughing heartily together creates lasting bonds. This is often expressed in positive feedback such as "*I haven't laughed like that in ages.*"

Conclusion

Working groups and teams are not the same thing! While working groups cooperate under central leadership, true teams largely organize themselves around the complex tasks at hand. Like improvisational theatre actors, members of such teams work together as an ensemble, with no permanent leader at the centre. Their constant striving to improve their collaboration is a central element to what makes them successful as a true team.

Successful teamwork can be brought about as follows:

- When participants disclose more about themselves, thus expanding the room for manoeuvre.
- Through mutual feedback, which shrinks the blind spot and leads to greater openness within the team.
- When everyone listens to each other and speaking time is evenly spread.
- When ideas, suggestions, and offers are respected, adopted, and taken further.
- When all team members are able to both take and relinquish the lead.
- When mistakes are acceptable.
- When conflicts are not swept under the carpet, but are brought out in the open.
- By building diversity into the team, and tapping into this diversity through openness and trust.

Applied improvisation can be used to build teams, weld them together, and prepare them for creative and innovative collaboration. If significant tension or open conflicts are present, alternative methods are more suitable.

Practical examples

Team development IBM

Main points

Company:
IBM is one of the world's leading companies for IT hardware, software, and services, and one of the largest consulting companies.

Assignment:
Team development through applied improvisation

Duration:
Two days

Target group:
Internal trainers from a management development unit

Goals:
The participants were to

- develop their individual spontaneity, flexibility, and creativity
- professionalize how they present themselves to groups, and their presence
- sharpen their perception of non-verbal communication
- broaden the scope of their abilities
- enhance their individual dynamism – and thus their effectiveness – as trainers
- learn how to use role-play in management seminars in a goal-oriented and practical way
- benefit from the joint experience to draw further together as a team

---

Initial situation and highlights

The customer was already familiar with applied improvisation, and wanted to use its methods. Given that the training was for a team from the area of management development, the workshop had several aims: on the one hand, the participants were to be given a boost for developing their own personalities, and on the other hand they were to enhance their professional expertise and their ability to lead. And not least, they were to come away with greater confidence to arrange their own seminars, and to grow closer together as a team.

A special feature of this workshop was an improvisational theatre show on the first evening, whereby the participants all came to the stage to improvise together. Naturally, everybody had a laugh too, and this further welded the team together. One of the games in this show was "Shortcuts." This exercise is very suitable for beginners, as it is easy to do, and everyone can take part, but only if they wish. Furthermore, the exercise requires good collaboration between participants.

Exercise

Shortcuts

Two players improvise a scene, until a third player calls out "*Freeze*." She then taps one of the players on the shoulder. That player leaves the stage, and a new scene begins. This scene may also be played out at a new location, but it is important that the new player can be quickly identified, whereas the first player maintains the character they started with. Each player has only one character, and can bring that character to the stage repeatedly. There are never more than two players on stage. Thus, the story is created and developed by all participants jointly.

Customer feedback from Felix Binggeli (GSS Leader Growth Markets):

Before the workshop, I had already had a lot to do with improvisational theatre, so I already knew the methods well. Since I had gained a lot from them even in my own training sessions, I decided to arrange an Impro Facilitation Workshop with our team of management development trainers. We wanted to use the workshop and methods from improv theatre to improve and expand our trainers' skills, and bring them closer together as a team.

With this training, we were really able to achieve both goals. Our trainers have become more creative, more daring, more ready to experiment, more spontaneous, and they also now use the methods in their own training sessions. Furthermore, the workshop was great for teambuilding, and that is exactly what I had wanted. It's amazing that we are still talking about that workshop, even though it was a few years ago now.

Team development "meinungsraum.at"

Main points

Company:
meinungsraum.at is an Austrian market research company with an emphasis on opinion polls and studying online markets.

Assignment:
Team development through applied improvisation

Duration:
Two days

Target group:
All of the company's staff

Goals:
The participants were to

- get to know each other better and strengthen the feeling that they are a member of the team
- learn about the "Yes, and . . ." principle as a key to teamwork and innovation
- professionalize how they present themselves to groups, and their presence
- enhance their ability to cope with unexpected and difficult situations in meetings
- increase their readiness to experiment and go out on a limb as part of the team

Initial situation and highlights

In 2012, the CEO of the Austrian company meinungsraum.at asked me to deliver a team development seminar for his staff, using applied improvisation. That first seminar generated a great deal of positive feedback in the team, leading to a follow-up seminar in 2014. Apart from a handful of new staff members, the participants were already familiar with the basics of improvisation from the first seminar. This meant that we could now go deeper, with more demanding and extensive exercises and themes.

A special feature of this workshop was that the participants were able to look at both the past and the future of the company, which they did through the following exercises:

Exercise

Looking back – bells and buzzer (adapted version)

In this exercise, a situation from the early days of an organization or company is reproduced. The founder or founders should be present. One of the founders is given a buzzer, and the other gets a bell (or a single founder gets both). The founders then broadly describe an important moment from the time they founded their organization, and specify who was there at the time. From the people present, they then decide who should play which role. Ideally, this should involve people who were not yet with the organization at that time. Those chosen then begin to "replay" the original situation. When the players do this more or less correctly, the bell is rung; when, however, they take the replay in the wrong direction, the buzzer is sounded. If necessary, the founders may make suggestions to get the players back on track.

This exercise is a good way to think back to the origins of the organization, and to revive the spirit that was there at the start.

As for looking to the future, the following exercise can help.

Exercise

Images of the future

The participants specify an occasion and a point in time, for example a Christmas party five years in the future. All teammates then improvise the scene as if everything has turned out exactly as hoped, and they talk about the successes of their business – for example takeovers, branches opened overseas, and new products developed. The dreams of all individual team members should be given space and accorded equal value.

The above exercise showed what all team members imagined and desired for the company. There may well have been ideas that could be implemented in reality. These chances to look into the past and the future of the company set the tone for the entire workshop.

Customer feedback from Herbert Kling (CEO):

The workshop in 2012 was meant as an incentive for my team. We figured it could be good to spend a day acting on stage together, and indeed we ended up in an actual theatre, a small underground one in Vienna, which was really atmospheric. By 2014, the company had made some big steps forward, and had almost doubled in size. This seemed to me another situation where I thought improv might be a good idea, but this time far more precisely focused. I wanted the team to consolidate and to get to know each other better. The workshop was fun, entertaining, and exciting. We got a lot out of it, particularly as regards the team members' understanding of each other.

I can still remember a really practical example. During the workshop, we did an Elevator Pitch exercise, with each person playing both a customer and a staff member of meinungsraum.at. The task was to briefly introduce the company, and this quickly brought to light something that nobody had seen before: the customer-facing staff had a complete overview of the company; the back-office people, however, simply couldn't explain what exactly we do and how we do it. After that, we developed our own programme that involved including the back-office staff in customer meetings and presentations.

This has had two lasting effects: first, the back-office personnel learned more about the company, especially about how complicated customers can be, and the extent to which the customer-facing staff shield the back office from that. Second, it changed the way we talk within the company: When we discover fundamental themes such as these, we use the term "improv effect," and we all know that we've come across something important.

Exercises for teamwork

1   Bells and Buzzer (adapted version)

Procedure: In this exercise, a situation from the early days of an organization or company is reproduced. The founder or founders should be present. One of the founders is given a horn, and the other gets a bell (or a single founder gets both). The founders then broadly describe an important moment from the time they founded their organization, and specify who was there at the time. From the people present, they then decide who should play which role. Ideally, this should involve people who were not yet with the organization at that time. Those chosen then begin to "replay" the original situation. When the players do this more or less correctly, the bell is rung; when, however, they take the replay in the wrong direction, the horn is sounded. If necessary, the founders may make suggestions to get the players back on track.

Themes:

Leading and allowing ourselves to be led: The lead is shared between the players on stage and the founders with their horn and bell.

Teamwork: Both sides must listen to each other and open up to the other in order to replay the situation as well as possible.

2   Counting to 21

Procedure: The group stands in a circle, and counts to 21. Each individual calls out numbers, but there is no fixed sequence of players, and whenever two individuals call out a number at the same time, the count must begin again from zero. This exercise is not about working out tricks, but about being fully focused on the teamwork and being in the here and now. The exercise shows very quickly how well the members of the team work together. Several rounds may be necessary, or indeed the exercise may not work out at all. Some teams, however, manage to get to 21 at the first attempt. Whatever the result, it can bring about valuable reflection on how the team works.

Themes:

> **Teamwork:** This exercise is only successful once everyone has forgotten about their own ego, and is giving their entire attention to the team.

> **Attention to the here and now:** Being right here in the moment is particularly important in this exercise.

3   Finding Things in Common

Procedure: All players stand in a circle. One player comes to the centre and says something about himself (e.g. "*I like hiking*"). All other players who have that in common then also come to the middle, and the others stay on the outside. Other possibilities may be "*I have a dog,*" "*I live in the countryside,*" "*I do like to be beside the seaside,*" and so on.

Themes:

> **Contact and getting to know one another**: This game is about getting to know each other better.

4   Humming Circle

Procedure: All players stand around the room, with their eyes closed. The trainer goes to the players and changes their position in the room, so that they become disoriented. The players then begin to hum, and should try to form a circle just by listening.

Themes:

> **Teamwork:** The players are only able to form a circle by listening to each other.

> **Attention to the here and now:** Here too it is vital to pay full attention.

5   Images of the Future

Procedure: The participants specify an occasion and a point in time, for example a Christmas party five years in the future. All teammates then improvise the scene as if everything has turned out exactly as hoped, and they talk about the successes of their business – for example takeovers, branches opened overseas, and new products developed. The dreams of all individual team members should be given space and accorded equal value.

Themes:

> **Accepting offers:** Other's ideas are accorded a "Yes, and . . .."

> **Co-creativity:** A joint vision of the future can be developed.

6   Leading the Blind

Procedure: The players form pairs. One player closes her eyes and lays her hand on the other, who then leads her around the room to various objects, which she can touch. After a while, the players swap places.

Themes:

> **Attention to the here and now:** Having the eyes closed can help a player keep their attention focused.

> **Leading and being led:** Both players must allow themselves to be led, and to lead the other.

7   **Name Swap**

Procedure: The players stand in a circle, then form pairs, so that the circle is now made up of pairs. One person goes into the middle. The pairs swap names; for example, Anna and Maria would now be Maria and Anna.

The person in the middle calls a name, and the person who (now) has that name must runs into the middle, while the other person in their pair tries to hold them in place.

Whoever makes a mistake has to come into the middle.

Themes:

> **Attention to the here and now**: This game requires great concentration.
>
> **Contact and getting to know one another**: In this game participants come physically closer to each other, and must even make physical contact.
>
> **Failing with good humour**: This game is most fun when people get it wrong!

8   **Shortcuts**

Procedure: Two players improvise a scene, until an audience member calls out "*Freeze.*" They then come on stage and tap one of the players on the shoulder. That player leaves the stage, and a new scene begins. This scene may also be played out at a new location, but it is important that the new player can quickly be identified, whereas the first player maintains the character they started with. Each player has only one character, and can bring that character to the stage repeatedly. There are never more than two players on stage. Thus, the story is created and developed by all participants jointly.

Themes:

> **Storytelling:** The participants work with each other to put a story together.
>
> **Co-creativity:** A meaningful story will only result if everyone cooperates.

9   **Spider's Web**

Procedure: All players stand in a circle, and imaginary webs will be strung out corresponding to words belonging to categories, such as countries, dishes, flowers, cars, and so on.

For example, in the first web, Player A says to Player D "*Italy*"; Player D says to Player B "*Portugal,*" and so on until every player has taken a turn. This web is then repeated in exactly the same order. Next, a second web is spun with another category, with new words being called out, in a different order. Then a third web is created using words from a third category, again in a different order. Finally, an attempt is made to get the participants to call out all three webs simultaneously by having them throw balls to each other in the same sequences as the three different webs.

Themes:

> **Attention to the here and now:** As soon as anyone loses concentration, the web will instantly fall apart.
>
> **Communication**: The players must listen carefully to each other and send their messages to the others.
>
> **Teamwork**: All players must cooperate for the exercise to work.

10 Swapping Stories

Procedure: The players form pairs, and tell each other a short personal story. They then swap pairs and repeat to their new partner the story they have just heard, telling the story as if it had happened to themselves, and using as many of the same words, gestures, and feelings as possible. This is repeated for several more rounds. Then all stand in a circle, and each relates the last story they heard.

Themes:

> **Attention to the here and now:** If somebody loses concentration, they cannot accurately repeat the details of the story.
>
> **Listening:** This exercise helps us not only to pay attention to the content, but also the body language and emotions.

11 What Comes Next?

Procedure: Two players stand on stage, and one begins with the words *"What comes next?"* Members of the audience then tell him what he should do or say. He follows the suggestions, then says *"What comes next?"* for the other player, and so on. The players only do or say what the audience members suggest, never blocking the offers.

The responsibility for the scene is handed over to the audience.

Themes:

> **Accepting offers:** An interesting scene can only be produced when the audience members' offers build on each other.
>
> **Leading and allowing ourselves to be led:** The players on stage must allow themselves to be led by the audience.
>
> **Making our partner look good:** Again, it is up to the audience to make suggestions that make the players on stage look good.
>
> **Teamwork:** Interesting scenes only come about through good cooperation within the audience.

12 What I Would Have Liked to Be!

Procedure: One player comes to the front and introduces himself before the group. In doing so, he should think about what he would have liked to have done in his life. Everything is possible; for example, he may have wanted to be the first human on Mars, an organic farmer with five kids, and so on. He introduces himself and relates all the details about his imaginary "other life," both professional and private. The themes should not be arbitrary; rather they should genuinely reflect a long-standing wish, a talent, an interest, etc. He should "pay homage" to these desires as he brings them on stage.

Themes:

> **Contact and getting to know one another**: This game is most suitable for groups whose participants already know each other well, as they will get to see new sides of their colleagues.

13   Word at a Time Story

Procedure: All players sit or stand in a circle, and attempt to tell a coherent story together, whereby each player may only say one word (or one line). The sequence continues repeatedly around the circle. Whenever the story begins to get tedious, any player may call time on it.

Themes:

> **Accepting offers:** The preceding offers must be accepted if the story is to have any meaning.
>
> **Leading and allowing ourselves to be led:** Players must be able to push the story forward, keep it running along, embellish it, or round it off.
>
> **Teamwork:** All must work together and build off each other's ideas.
>
> **Failing with good humour:** If the story fails, it can be killed off at any time.

Bibliography

Edmondson, A. (2013). *Teaming to innovate*. San Francisco: Bass & Wiley.

Halpern, C., Close, D., and Johnson, H. K. (1994). *Truth in comedy – The manual of improvisation*. Colorado Springs: Meriwether.

Luft, J. (1963). *Einführung in die Gruppendynamik*. Stuttgart: Klett.

Online sources

Duhigg, C. (2016). What google learned from its quest to build the perfect team. *The New York Times Magazine*. Available at: www.nytimes.com/2016/02/28/magazine/what-google-learned-from-its-quest-to-build-the-perfect-team.html?_r=0 [Accessed 29 May 2018].

Chapter 5

Creativity

Introduction to creativity

Few words today are so glamorous and carry as much weight as "creativity." Everyone talks about it, everybody claims to have it, and anyone who does not offer it should expect to lose out in the competition for products and talents – and this applies to companies, staff, politicians, or even private individuals. Naturally, this places great pressure on people and companies, and ironically enough, this pressure jeopardizes the very quality of creativity it is supposed to bring about. Being creative to order is every bit as impossible as being spontaneous to order. These two characteristics have much in common, as we can see when we watch children playing, for example.

Indeed, we were born creative. Without our enormous creativity, we humans would never have survived as a species. We would never have learned to tame fire, which gave us a richer diet, which in turn allowed our brains to grow. We would never have invented the wheel, the internal combustion engine, electricity, computers, and so on.

Figure 5.1 © Evi Fill

Today, change and innovation are everywhere, and are becoming increasingly complex, and more and more people are feeling overwhelmed. Creativity is one way we can stop ourselves from drowning, as it helps us cope with uncertainty and complexity. Creativity leads not only to new technologies, but also to the ability to solve the problems caused by these same new technologies and the changed societal conditions they bring about.

The key to this is the harmonization or at least the tolerance of contrasts. Stephen Nachmanovitch (1990) presents this ability as one of the central definitions of creativity, writing: *"Creativity is the harmony of opposite tensions."* (Nachmanovitch, 1990, p. 12)

Examples of such tensions are:

- Simplicity versus complexity
- Structure versus chaos
- Individual versus collective
- Homogeneity versus diversity
- Consciousness versus the unconscious
- Having ideas versus letting ideas go
- Error avoidance versus making mistakes

In their work, improvisational theatre actors must be able to reconcile and unite all these contradictions. Such actors are simultaneously authors and directors, creating new worlds on stage at the spur of the moment. And the fact that improvisational theatre does not allow for rehearsal means that these actors' training is essentially formed around the development of creative ability. Applied improvisation offers a rich source of as-yet little-known experiences, theories, and exercises around the subject of creativity.

With these tools of applied improvisation, and from the standpoint of research into creativity, this chapter looks at the following basic questions:

- Are we all creative?
- What is the difference between creativity and innovation?
- What are convergent and divergent thinking?
- Does being creative take time?
- Can we structure creativity?
- What is co-creativity?
- Which methods can we use to foster creativity?
- How should we deal with mistakes?

Let it be said already that there are no simple answers to these questions. If we wish to be creative, we must be ready to live with uncertainty.

Being creative

Whereas in the past it was assumed that creativity was the exclusive domain of a handful of geniuses, since the middle of the 20th century the perception that all people are creative has been gaining ground. The psychologist Joy Paul Guilford was one of the first to apply scientific arguments to this assumption, thus paving the way for today's research into creativity.

Many people are convinced that they possess little or no creative ability. Children, however, do not even give this a second thought – they are creative, period. This is because they still have full access to their unconscious, they automatically accept offers, and they are not yet in the habit of evaluating themselves and others to the extent adults do. Insecurity and doubt regarding our own creativity only emerge once we start being evaluated by others. It is the fear of being evaluated that blocks us, rather than any lack of creativity in itself.

Paul Z. Jackson (2015), the founder of the Applied Improvisation Network, believes that the majority of new ideas are initially criticized, and thus that we should not be surprised when most people give up sharing their ideas, and over time will not even "share" their ideas with themselves. This will naturally lead to people claiming not to be creative.

Still not convinced? Then consider your dreams. In our dreams we can build fantastic worlds and discover astounding connections. And even if many of us cannot even remember our own dreams, they remain a bubbling pot for our creativity. Our fears are another example of our own creativity, as we can be extraordinarily inventive when we imagine that something terrible has happened, or is about to happen. Indeed, the very people who claim to lack creativity can often be masters in the art of evoking magnificent fantasies based on fear. And fantasy is creativity!

An excellent exercise on this comes from the founder of modern improvisational theatre, Keith Johnstone (1981). He calls for someone to come up on stage, and asks them to take an imaginary book down from an imaginary bookcase. The person should then give the title of the book, and describe it (shape, colour, material, etc.). They are then asked to "read out" a sentence from the book. Almost everyone manages to do this, thus demonstrating creativity. The success of this exercise is due to the way it is built up gradually, thus preventing the person becoming overwhelmed and falling prey to self-criticism.

Creativity and innovation

The terms "creativity" and "innovation" are frequently used interchangeably; however they do not mean the same thing. "Creativity" comes from the Latin stem "creare," meaning "bring about, invent or make something new." "Innovation" is from the Latin verb "innovare," which can be understood as "renewing" or taking creative ideas further. We only start talking about innovation once a product, service or process is implemented, used successfully, and brought to the market.

Min Basadur (1994), an engineer and scientist known for his research into the subject of "applied creativity," describes innovation processes as having three phases:

Phase 1: Problem formulation
Phase 2: Solution formulation
Phase 3: Solution implementation

Each of these three phases is split into an idea (creativity) and a judgement of that idea (evaluation). Thus, innovation goes beyond creativity, and can require somewhat different abilities and conditions.

Taking this idea further, Harvard professor Amy Edmondson (2013) believes that innovation demands meaningful goals that will truly motivate teams – goals that are not only profit-oriented, but that go towards making the world a better place. This condition makes it possible for staff to get behind the project and be creative.

Convergent and divergent thinking

In today's business world, companies need to plan in the long term, and make the future as foreseeable and predictable as they can. According to Joy Paul Guilford, this goal-oriented approach and rational-logical thinking may also be termed "convergent thinking." "Convergere" is Latin for "lean towards each other," so this type of thinking allows more precise planning and the achievement of established goals.

However, creative processes also require divergent thinking. Divergence (Latin: "divergere") means "striving away from each other," and is necessary for developing alternatives, and exploring all possibilities. This type of "tending away from each other within a framework of friendship" does not constrict, and does not reduce complexity; rather, it opens up space. This will initially increase diversity and complexity, which is a necessary part of venturing outside of the familiar, to take steps into the unknown.

This process will strike fear into many people's hearts. They will then quickly activate the rational-logical thinking that with a simple "Yes, but . . ." can stop divergent thinking in its tracks. We are all familiar with such situations: someone expresses an unusual idea, and is immediately stonewalled and rejected through a flurry of "Yes, but . . ." comments. Such a reaction can be extremely demotivating, and will hinder any future attempts in this direction.

Divergent thinking can be practised through the "Metamorphosis" exercise from improvisational theatre:

Exercise

Metamorphosis

All players stand in a circle, and pass an object to each other. Each person must use the object in a different way. Let us say the object is a scarf: for Player A it may be a snake, and Player A passes it on to Player B as a snake. Then for Player B it may be a flying carpet, and so on.

Creativity and time

A common view is that creativity is triggered spontaneously. An incredible discovery striking us like an apple to the head, a beautiful melody that simply comes to us while we are out on a walk, or a poem popping into our minds as we watch the sunset; but in reality, creativity is a process that takes time.

Social psychologist Graham Wallas (1926) suggested a four-phase model for the creative process:

Phase 1: Preparation
Phase 2: Incubation
Phase 3: Illumination
Phase 4: Verification

After a preparation phase, in the incubation phase we intentionally distance ourselves from problems to allow our unconscious to work on them. In the illumination phase we hope for creative ideas, which we can then test during the verification phase.

In improvisational theatre this process must happen extremely quickly, because the players on stage have no time to spare, and must be instantly creative. This means that the preparation phase must already have taken place during training, when spontaneity is practised. During training, improv players learn to dismantle self-criticism and repress the urge to be funny or original, which allows them freer access to their unconscious. On stage, these abilities must all be immediately accessible, so that the actors can be "enlightened" with new ideas. The verification phase is run through the audience: every player will be acutely attuned to the audience's reaction, whether they laugh, show amazement, puzzlement, or boredom.

In a company setting, creativity must be given time, without pressure. Here, though, a new obstacle rears its head: an objection applying to any company today – "Time is money."

Creativity and structure

Several phase models attempt to structure the creative process. Very popular right now is the "**Design Thinking Model**" developed by computer scientists Terry Winograd, Larry Leifer and David Kelly, and including elements from the Wallas model. Design Thinking takes the sequence from the classic Wallas model, and expands it with the element of collective work in teams.

The phases of this model are as follows:

*   **Empathize:** understand the problem
*   **Define:** analyse, interpret, and plan
*   **Ideate:** imagine, research, ponder
*   **Prototype:** apply creativity to create
*   **Test:** review and revise

All such process models attempt to structure the creative process, make it plannable, and somehow tie it down and bring form to the chaos of creativity. Design

Thinking – again, like all such models – attempts to simplify complexity, and is thus often useful for companies, but at the same time somewhat limited. Experienced artists hardly ever work with processes such as these, as they would restrict the artists' creativity. But the less experienced a person is with accessing creativity, the more support these process models appear to give.

Co-creativity

Many books on the subject of creativity, and much research into it, tend to talk about the creativity of the individual. Only in the last few years has research turned increasingly towards co-creativity. Despite the myth, the fact is that very few innovations spring from the mind of an individual "genius." In general, they will have built on existing experience and knowledge, effectively deploying the improvisational theatre tactic of "Yes, and . . .." Furthermore, most cases of "genius" – or indeed creativity – will have crucially involved several people, who will often have remained in the background.

Alexander Haslam and his colleagues at the University of Groningen have carried out research that demonstrates how creativity principally arises from dynamic group processes, rather than representing a characteristic of gifted individuals.

> Artists, authors and natural scientists often achieve their most creative work when they collaborate with one or more other people – with friends, colleagues or contemporaries who are of the same mind.
> (www.wiwo.de/erfolg/trends/kreativitaet-genies-sind-keine-einzelgaenger/8946456.html, accessed 29 May 2018)

This theory was further confirmed by studies carried out over the last decade (Haslam et al., 2013).

Although most innovative developments have involved many people, we still tend to attach only individual "geniuses" to these events. Or can you still remember who collaborated with Steve Jobs to found Apple, or with Mark Zuckerberg to create Facebook?

Co-creativity and diversity

Psychologist and engineer Amy Edmondson (2013) of Harvard University has spent a long time researching teamwork, creativity, and innovation. She highlights how innovation is a team sport requiring collaboration to expand the boundaries of knowledge. She lays out the following preconditions for a team to be creative and for innovation to occur:

- Effective teamwork requires all team members to be open to and interested in the others' needs, abilities, interests, and goals, independently of their position in the hierarchy.

- The goal of any teamwork is to integrate different perspectives to give rise to new solutions.
- For this, participants need affective abilities (feelings) and cognitive abilities (thinking).
- Teams and companies must live with paradoxes, e.g. play versus discipline, high standards versus a tolerance for errors, specialists versus generalists.
- Mistakes must be uncovered and addressed early, so that lessons may be learned.

Psychologist and professor at the University of Bremen Peter Kruse (1997) also believes that creativity can no longer be the preserve of individuals in today's complex world. In these times of global commercial and communication networks, it is increasingly important to deploy systems that are as complex and dynamic as the market itself. This complexity is driven by increased diversity. Kruse writes that creativity requires systems that contain frictions that generate phases of instability, which in turn enables a transition to new patterns.

We can see that we no longer come far if we try to walk alone, and we need to have in place the conditions necessary for co-creativity.

Recognition of teamwork

If a team is to be creative (i.e. co-creative), it is crucial to acknowledge the performance of the whole team, rather than of individuals. Without this, there will be little motivation to genuinely commit to a team, to open up, and to be creative together. Individuals will then prefer to take their own ideas directly to the boss, or they will go and use their ideas in their own start-up business.

At the European Organization for Nuclear Research (CERN), all publications list the names of all participants in alphabetical order, irrespective of their individual contribution. This applies even to winners of the Nobel Prize (Beglinger, 2013), and is an example of how all staff can be recognized, their motivation strengthened, and true teamwork brought about. In the trickiest cases, teams are indeed more creative together than an individual could possibly be, which is why team creativity or co-creativity is also more effective for complex problems. Furthermore, it will boost the team's acceptance and their commitment when it comes to implementation.

From "Yes, but . . ." to "Yes, and . . ."

Already back in 1939, American author and ad man Alex F. Osborn observed how negative thinking ran through meetings. He noticed how often phrases such as "out of the question," "impossible," or simply "no" were used, and how they hindered any creativity. His remedy was to develop the oldest and best-known creativity technique: brainstorming. Vital to this technique is that nobody has exclusive rights to ideas – that all ideas belong to everybody. This allows participants to build more easily on the ideas of others, and thus represents a perfect example of a "Yes, and . . ." exercise. Unfortunately, this ideal form of brainstorming is rarely implemented; rather, each individual will bring his own existing ideas to the table in the hope that his ideas will be judged "the best," and will be taken further. An experiment by social psychologist Sven F. Goergens (2009) found that 20 people reflecting individually on a problem generated up to 50 per cent more original ideas than "teams" using this "hidden competitive" form of brainstorming. As long as ideas continue to be attributed to individuals, and thus cannot be built upon by others, nothing new can be created by a team!

Listening to others' ideas, picking them up, and building on them – the "Yes, and . . ." principle – is a precondition for any creative work within a team. The "Yes, and . . ." may be in the form of an attitude, or may be explicitly spoken. Thinking originally and bringing in new perspectives is possible and necessary, but only if participants pick up others' ideas and run with them, rather than shooting them down.

Saying "No" and offering criticism is also necessary, but only after the creativity phase, when the ideas move into the evaluation phase to be sorted and developed. Ideally, by this stage ideas can no longer be attributed to individuals, but will have become joint ideas owned by everybody. This also means that criticism of an idea no longer affects individual team members or makes them feel undervalued.

Methods for fostering creativity

Separating the generation and evaluation of ideas

In creative processes, it is essential to separate the phase where ideas are generated from the phase where they are evaluated. For true creativity, there should initially be no evaluation, either negative or positive, as even a positive judgement can hinder creativity, for example when only the contributions of certain individuals receive attention, because they are "creative," and are thus evaluated positively.

In principle, the core of creative work is very simple: to be able to be creative, we need to be able to access our unconscious. And to have that access, we must feel safe, and must be confident that our own ideas will not be automatically denigrated, even implicitly.

Only *after* the creative process do we come to the analysis and selection phases. At this point, of course, ideas do need to be evaluated and filtered. Now the word "No" may be used, to indicate which new ideas and concepts are or are not usable or capable of being implemented, and which should be dropped or taken further.

Accessing our unconscious

How do we "access" our unconscious, though? In his foreword to Keith Johnstone's book *Improvisation and the Theatre* (1981, p. 11), the English writer and theatre critic Irving Wardle wrote:

> Switch off the no-saying intellect and welcome the unconscious as a friend: it will lead you to places you never dreamed of, and produce results more original than anything you could achieve by aiming at originality.

Many creative ideas spring from the unconscious. Accessing it is really only possible when we are not observing and monitoring ourselves. We must also accept our own offers, and this is not quite as natural as we might think! The exercise "Association Circle" is a great way to try this out.

Exercise

Association circle

The players stand in a circle and the first player says a word, for example "flower," and the second player must say the first word that comes into her head, for example "water," and so on round the circle.

There will always be some players who hesitate longer before saying their word. Although each player makes an immediate association, this first idea will frequently *not* be expressed in public. There are several reasons for this:

Originality: We do not think our first thought is original or funny enough.
Sexuality: The idea is of a sexual nature, so we censor it.
Opening up: The idea is too personal, and we are afraid of revealing too much about ourselves.

Figure 5.2 © Evi Fill

When these fears lead us to suppress the first thought that comes into our heads, we may end up saying the third or fourth, which leads to hesitation. We thus disrupt the flow of creativity, not only for ourselves, but for the others.

This is why there are many exercises in improvisational theatre designed to steer us away from this self-monitoring. We may use mantras, for example. The audience gives each player a mantra, such as "*I love all people*," or "*I can do this*," and the players must constantly repeat this to themselves throughout the scene. This "outsmarting ourselves" is a very effective way to evade being inhibited by self-monitoring. As it happens, this exercise can also be very useful in other challenging or difficult situations. For example, the mantra "*Everything is going to be alright*" works well in job interviews, and "*I can do this*" is good for presentations.

The British comedian John Cleese, who paid a great deal of attention to creativity, calls this state "open mode," as opposed to "closed mode." He is effectively talking about "Flow," which in his eponymous book the psychologist Mihály Csíkszentmihályi (1996) describes as an open and trancelike state during which ideas can flow freely. This flow state is often evident in creative processes, and the people involved find it to be extremely liberating.

Developing creative ideas

Improvisational theatre offers us many different approaches and exercises to help us develop creative ideas.

Association

(Free) association links conscious and unconscious thoughts together. These associations facilitate our access to our unconscious, thus allowing an unhindered flow of thought.

In improvisational theatre we have many exercises to practise association, for example:

Exercise

Associations

A player comes to the stage and the audience calls out words to him. For each word, he should make an association and express it as quickly as possible. An alternative approach is for him to come up with as many associations as possible for one word in one minute. An additional twist may be for him to use only nouns, verbs, and so on.

By using associations we can give ourselves more room around the problem, and trigger our imagination to find new solutions.

Thinking in images

Thinking in images is seeing our thoughts as pictures. It is a step away from logical-rational thinking, and is another way to give ourselves more space and flexibility.

The following exercise, "I am a tree," can help with thinking in images.

Exercise

I am a tree

All players stand in a circle. One player moves to the centre and says, for example, "*I am a tree*." A second player joins her and says, for example, "*I am a squirrel on the tree*." A third player may then say something like, "*I am a nut*." Each player tries to expand the image, and there are never more than three players on stage. Then the first player takes one of the others with her, saying, "*I'm taking the squirrel with me*," or "*I'm taking the nut with me*," and those two players go back out to stand in the circle. The player left in the middle now repeats what he is, for example, "*I am a nut*." Two new players come in and repeat the process, thus building a new picture, and so on.

Thinking in images can open up completely new and unusual perspectives to help us solve problems.

Forming analogies

We can use analogies to associate similar things in new ways. Once again, this opens up new possibilities for us, as we find analogies and similarities in other areas, which we can then apply to our current problems.

Here is an exercise from improvisational theatre:

Exercise

Making links

One player stands in the centre, with two other players next to him. The two players call out a word to him, and he must try to find a link between these two words. For example, "plaster" and "looroll": "*If you scrape the plaster from the walls, you can make great looroll from it*." The links do not have to be realistic; the idea is to foster the ability to form analogies.

When we apply this to a concrete problem, we attempt to place this problem in another context and look for solutions there.

Changing perspectives

The ability to change perspectives means being able to put ourselves inside the thoughts and feelings of another. Taking on such new perspectives lets us develop new ideas.

For this, improvisational theatre offers us the Perspectives Game.

Exercise

Perspectives game

A problem is introduced and briefly described. Three players then come to the front of the stage, and must take on three roles given to them by the audience. Unusual perspectives may be applied – for example, a player may demonstrate a product. All three players then take turns to present their perspective on the problem. Whenever a player begins to speak, the other two must be quiet, as it is important that all three perspectives be accorded the same amount of time.

In this way, problems can be illuminated from different sides, to make possible solutions easier to see.

Letting ideas go

If there is one thing that may be more difficult than coming up with our own ideas, it is letting our own ideas go. But this is exactly what we need to do if we wish to be creative in a team. We often hold onto our own ideas, to the exclusion of anything new or unfamiliar; after all, who knows where that could lead?

One of the main principles of improvisational theatre is being able to let our ideas go. For example, a player comes to the stage intending to play a school-teacher, but if the other players cannot recognize this, and say, "*Mum, what's for dinner?*", then the first player must be ready to throw out her original idea. Another example: one player thinks she is dealing with a problematic teenager, and says, "*And just how late was it last night?*" The other player, however, has a different idea of the situation, and answers, "*But Mum, I didn't read for much longer.*" Once again, the first player has to abandon her initial plan, and start in with a brand-new idea.

In creative teamwork, the ability to let go of our own ideas is almost more important than actually having our own ideas. Once again, this is about not seeing ourselves as the centre of the universe, but rather investing in the group. This type of narcissism is not so easy to shake off.

Dealing with mistakes

In many areas, it is highly important to avoid making mistakes as much as possible, for example on the road, or piloting an aircraft. Avoiding mistakes implies self-control, but where creativity is concerned, too much self-control can be an obstacle. The freedom to make mistakes without being punished enables us to experiment and take risks, and is vital to innovation.

> Anyone who has never made a mistake has never tried anything new.
> (Albert Einstein)

Since the beginning of the 20th century, scientists have been delving deeply into the subject of "mistakes": how we should view them, what their effect is, and what opportunities they present. In the 1970s we began to concern ourselves systematically with the subject not only in the pedagogical context, but also in business. In the 1990s, the themes of "innovative learning" and "learning organizations" began to appear in management literature. Eventually, innovative companies started viewing "mistakes" in the context of a culture of error tolerance, and consciously made use of them through tolerance and openness to non-standard approaches.

Many researchers today believe that a productive culture of error tolerance is necessary in organizations. However, what this should actually look like remains the subject of much debate. Educators, for example, attempt to create a climate that is free of fear, and which allows people to learn from mistakes. In contrast, quality managers must still try to eliminate mistakes, to ensure the highest quality levels possible. Innovation managers, in their turn, see mistakes rather as an opportunity, and thus are very open to them.

The "two truths" model

The different viewpoints above may be better understood by applying the "two truths" model. Originally a Platonic concept, the idea was further developed by Gerhard Schwarz (2003). The "first truth" speaks of rules and regulations – which in companies may be standards and best practices – as a basis for decision-making. Difficulties in applying these rules are seen as errors and deviations that need to be reined in by the application of controls. Developing new rules aimed at eliminating such errors may be the task of a quality manager, for example.

The "second truth" concerns decisions that cannot be based on existing rules, precisely because these rules do not yet exist. These are situations in which contradictions come to the surface, and which are changeable and fluid. In today's complex business environment of increasingly demanding products, processes, and organizational relationships, there is less and less chance that the "right" approach is clearly the "best" solution from the very start. This means that in this "second truth," communication is needed to admit novelty and uncertainty, to address the (necessary) contradictions and confusions, and to factor in the feelings and emotions of those concerned.

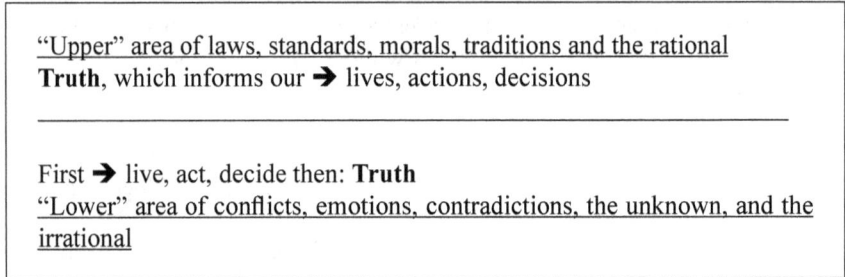

"Upper" area of laws, standards, morals, traditions and the rational
Truth, which informs our ➜ lives, actions, decisions

First ➜ live, act, decide then: **Truth**
"Lower" area of conflicts, emotions, contradictions, the unknown, and the irrational

---

Figure 5.3 The "two truths" model

When it comes to finding creative solutions for complex problems and developing new products, when we are effectively inventing the future, then there is no right and wrong. This perspective is above all characteristic of innovation managers and representatives of learning organizations.

Not apportioning blame

A primary cause of people's fear of making mistakes is the reflex reaction to look for who to blame and punish when something goes wrong. We all learned this fear already in school, and most of us found it all over again in our professional lives.

However, mistakes are a vital part of the creative process, and being afraid of making mistakes inhibits that process. In improvisational theatre we say that you cannot be a good improv actor if you no longer fail, because this means that you are no longer pushing the envelope and taking risks; you have ceased to be truly creative, and are merely repeating the tried and trusted approaches.

Amy Edmondson (2013) also looked at the theme of failure, and developed the following matrix.

Table 1 A Spectrum of Potential Causes of Organizational Failures. (Edmondson, 2013, p. 82; courtesy of Wiley)

Potential cause of failure		Is blame appropriate?
Deliberate violation	An individual chooses to violate a prescribed process or practice.	Yes
Inattention	An individual inadvertently deviates from a prescribed process or practice.	Maybe

Potential cause of failure		Is blame appropriate?
Lack of ability	An individual does not have the skills, conditions, or training to execute a job.	Unlikely
Inadequate process	An individual adheres to a prescribed process, but the process is faulty or incomplete.	Unlikely
Task challenge	An individual faces a task that is too difficult to be executed reliably every time.	Doubtful
Complexity	A process composed of many elements breaks down when novel interactions take place.	Rarely
Uncertainty	Lacking sufficient knowledge of future events, people take reasonable actions that nonetheless produce undesired results.	No
Hypothesis-testing experiment	An experiment conducted to test a prediction that a particular design or course of action will produce a particular result fails to confirm the hypothesis.	No
Exploratory experiment	An experiment conducted to expand knowledge and investigate a possibility leads to an undesired result.	No

As the matrix very clearly shows, apportioning blame becomes increasingly inappropriate as the tasks at hand increase in complexity. On this scale, creative processes belong very near the bottom.

Failing with good humour in improvisational theatre

In improvisational theatre, we speak of "failing with good humour." In other words, failure should not simply be "tolerated"; it is actually *desirable*, and ideally should even be fun. In good teamwork on stage, we always try to make the most of failures, to get the best out of them. After all, making mistakes is not only a learning opportunity, but also a chance to create something new. James Joyce put it like this: "Mistakes are the portals of discovery," and thus a crucial element in creative processes.

It is no surprise, then, that mistakes and failures are welcome in improvisational theatre. One example comes from Kat Koppett (2001, p. 38). This scene took place on stage at Bay Area Theatresports, and involves a divorced couple fighting over who should get custody of the children. During the fight, the ex-wife suddenly pulls an imaginary pistol out of her bag, and points it at her ex-husband.

The ex-husband blocks the "offer," saying, "*What's that in your hand, anyway? That's not a gun.*"

The ex-wife answers, "*It is a gun. I put a milk carton over it so that it wouldn't scare the kids.*"

Figure 5.4 © Evi Fill

In doing this, she accepts his block and continues to build the scene around her offer (the gun) and his block.

We can see how this leads to new, original ideas as our team heads down the less-travelled path leading to new and creative solutions.

Successful failure at "The Second City"

The Second City is the most successful comedy stage and improv school in the United States. In their book "Yes, And – Lessons from The Second City" (2015), Kelly Leonard and Tom Yorton list their six best ways to fail:

To fail in public

People are most afraid of failing in public. But only in public can ideas be assessed on the spot, improving collaboration. Failing in public is the fastest way to throw light on mistakes.

Companies just starting up have now begun to deploy new strategies whereby they communicate their ideas to a great number of people so as to receive immediate feedback on whether the ideas could be implemented. This same strategy is also a basis for "agile software development," which involves bringing the client into the software development process as early as possible, once again with the aim of uncovering bugs at an early stage.

The Second City always tests its new comedy pieces in front of a real audience, to find out what makes people laugh and pay attention, and which parts tend to fall flat. Thus, in their work with companies they also advise bringing customer feedback into the innovation process as early as possible.

To fail together

To be able to learn from "failing in public" we must be prepared to consider it as "failing together." This involves resisting the urge to get ourselves out of the situation and stand at the edge, to instead – and this is completely in contrast – jump into the scene to drag our colleagues out of the mess and help the whole team develop the story further. Being ready to fail together is fundamental to joint success. In the same way that good ideas rarely spring from just one person, mistakes cannot usually be ascribed to any one individual.

To fail fast

Failing fast means, on the one hand, noticing quickly when something is going wrong. And on the other hand, it means putting the mistake behind us as quickly as possible, and moving on. The sooner a mistake is recognized, the less serious the consequences tend to be.

To fail free of judgement

The actors at The Second City try not to look for guilty parties when somebody messes up. This facilitates a culture in which experiments can be made, risks taken, and where unusual and confusing situations are welcome. This, in turn, allows mistakes to be turned to the good.

To fail with confidence

Failing with confidence means failing without losing our trust in ourselves, and believing that mistakes can lead to successes and unconventional ideas.

To fail incrementally

In good teamwork, something new is being created through the work of all concerned; step-by-step, each person is bringing in their contributions. In the same way, any individual's mistake should not then bring the whole thing crashing down.

Dealing with mistakes in training sessions

When we use methods from improvisational theatre in training sessions, we attempt to create an atmosphere in which participants are not afraid of making mistakes. A good exercise for this is Whisky Mixer.

Exercise

Whisky mixer

All players stand in a circle and pass words to each other. The phrase "Whisky Mixer" is passed to the right, and the phrase "Mister Whisker" goes to the left. With the phrase "Misty Vista," a player can change the direction of the game. The most important rule is that anyone who cannot help laughing has to run once round the outside of the circle. Bloopers or incorrect words do not actually matter, so the real "mistake" in the game is to laugh.

This exercise helps people feel that making mistakes is part of the game, and that it can even be fun. Naturally, part of this is that the trainer will also make mistakes, and laugh about them. This is why it is a good idea for trainers themselves to join in with exercises and mess up along with the participants.

Conclusion

Creativity is like a cat: it comes and goes, is not too interested in anything we have to say, and does not like to be tied down – but if we handle it properly, it gives a lot back to us.

We may try to measure creativity, to structure it and plan it, but all this is scarcely possible.

There are ways to foster creativity. To do this, we need the following:

- the security of knowing we can tolerate uncertainty and contradiction
- enough time to work without pressure
- access to our unconscious
- teams, as these are more creative than individuals, provided they truly work together and the members accept each other's offers
- diversity, to throw different light on problems and to be able to work with complexity
- an atmosphere in which team performance is acknowledged
- the freedom to make mistakes without being penalized

Finally, since there are no simple answers for this subject – as has already been mentioned – it is now up to you to draw your own conclusions!

Practical examples

Symposium on the subject of creativity for an art school

Main points

Company:
The Art School in St. Gallen, Switzerland, is a not-for-profit association that nurtures creative expression in children and young people.

Assignment:
Introduction to the subject of creativity, with practical exercises for all participants

Duration:
30 minutes

Target group:
80 participants in the symposium

Goals:
The participants were to

- become motivated and fired up for the subject of the symposium
- learn about the "Yes, and . . ." principle as a key to creative collaboration
- get creative themselves, with the help of short exercises

INITIAL SITUATION AND HIGHLIGHTS

In 2016, the Art School, together with the School for Design, organized a symposium on the subject of creativity at the School for Design in St. Gallen.

A colleague and I were invited to warm the audience up after the opening, to loosen them up and to get them ready to tackle the subject. We felt it was important to get the audience as active as possible. We were somewhat restricted by the fact that the audience was seated in rows, so we had to work around that.

We began by **warming up** together. We asked all participants to stand up and introduce themselves to their neighbours. We then got them all to skip on the spot with an imaginary skipping rope. To finish the warmup, we came to who was allowed to sit down again – first, only those who came by car, then those who came by train, and finally all those in a relationship. This meant that the only people left standing were those who came on foot or by bicycle (i.e. those who lived locally), and who were single – which was a nice chance for those people to get to know each other.

For the main part of the training, we focused on three dramatic themes:

- accepting offers
- being in the moment
- making our partner look good

We offered some input for each of these themes. After we had demonstrated a suitable exercise on stage, the participants could try out the exercise with their neighbour.

One exercise on the technique of "accepting offers" was as follows:

Exercise

Giving presents

This exercise requires two players. One player hands the other an imaginary object, and says, "*I brought you a present!*" In doing so, he should try to "mime" the size and weight of the gift.

The other player unwraps it and replies, "*Oh, thank you, it's a . . .,*" and should try to work out what it is from the clues given by the first player.

To close the training, my colleague and I gave a short improvisational theatre performance, to show the audience how we work together creatively on stage, and how we might fail with good humour.

Customer feedback from Lucia Andermatt, Claudia Sturzengger, and Silja D'Agostino (Art School):

It was important for us to "activate" the participants at the start of our symposium, to get them fired up and spark a creative mood in their heads, hearts, and bodies. This wish led us to the idea of using improvisational theatre.

We were stunned to see how quickly many people got moving, how the rigid structure got broken up, how people loosened up, how their faces lit up, and their "concentration" was replaced by smiles all around.

The "accepting offers" exercise kicked things off. At first, we were still a little shy with our neighbours, but then we were always pleasantly surprised by the unexpected reaction of the other person. In "making our partner look good" we were to give our partner some positive feedback, and to make compliments. The at times ambiguous and amusing situations helped to "reset" our grey matter to "open and ready."

We could all clearly see that so many things are possible, and that we are capable of accepting or creating novelty. The mood that was established at the start set a great foundation for the whole day of the symposium. This contribution switched all our senses on!

Workshop "School for Design"

Main points

Company:
The School for Design in St. Gallen is the main centre for training in visual communication and creative arts in eastern Switzerland.

Assignment:
Opening event for the start of the visual communication and interactive media design courses

Duration:
1.5 days

Target group:
All participants in these two courses

Goals:
The participants were to

- get to know each other, establish a firm basis for learning and working together
- build up courage and self-confidence for a good start to the course
- learn to take on responsibility for themselves and others in order to generate a creative environment
- learn about the "Yes, and . . ." principle as a key to creative collaboration
- try new things and expand their sphere of activity

INITIAL SITUATION AND HIGHLIGHTS

The School for Design runs their courses on "Visual Communication" and "Interactive Media Design" on a two-year cycle. All students are expected to work very closely together, both within their own course and with students of the other course. The course director wanted all participants to meet each other right at the start of the first semester, so that they would quickly be comfortable working together in an atmosphere of creativity and cooperation.

In our workshop on co-creativity, we focused on the following themes:

- Openness and trust in contact with one another (Johari Window)
- Accepting offers ("Yes, and . . .")
- Attention to the here and now
- Failing with good humour

At the end of the workshop my colleague and I got the participants to prepare role-plays on the subject of "**A class reunion 10 years from now**." We asked them to think about what they would be happy about 10 years in the future, what they would be proud of, and what memories they would like to have. These role-plays were filmed so that the students could look back at them at the end of their courses.

Customer feedback from Kathrin Lettner (Head of Further Education, School for Design, St. Gallen):

Given that we offer further education in the field of creative design, I naturally wanted to start the courses off with a bang. I had two ideas in my mind: I wanted to sow the seeds in a way that the students would remember, and I wanted to spark good cooperation between the courses. The workshop met both of these expectations.

The courses started with a great deal of positive energy, and the participants felt right at home. They are still energized by the workshop, as I could see in their midterm grades. I did not attend the workshop myself; nor was I able to see the films of the role-plays, as we plan to wait until the graduation party – that is, after three years – to show them. In this way, the students and I will be equally excited and certainly surprised when we see the films.

Exercises on the theme of creativity

1   An Important Invention

Procedure: This exercise requires four or five players. One player starts by talking about an invention that is important for the company. The scene should then continue with a series of "*Yes, exactly, and . . ..*" For example:

Player A: "*We really need something that makes our work less boring.*"
Player B: "*Yes, exactly, and we write a computer programme for that.*"
Player C: "*Yes, exactly, and this programme can answer all our emails for us.*"
Player D: "*Yes, exactly, and it always expresses things in just the right way.*"
Player E: "*Yes, exactly, and it can even read our emails and add all the important information to my calendar.*"
. . . and so on.

Themes:

Accepting offers: The players work together on this invention, and must always accept the previous player's offer.

Co-creativity: Collaboration is vital to uncover new ways and ideas.

2 **Association Circle**

Procedure: All players stand in a circle. One player calls out a word, and the player to her right calls out the first word that comes into his head, and so on around the circle.

Themes:

Creativity: Free association is a crucial ability for any creativity.

Accessing the unconscious: This exercise should happen very quickly, so that the players have no time to think, and really say the very first word that comes to mind.

3 **Associations**

Procedure: A player comes to the stage and the audience calls out words to him. For each word, he should make an association and express it as quickly as possible. An alternative approach is for him to come up with as many associations as possible for one word in one minute. An additional twist may be for him to use only nouns, verbs, and so on.

Themes:

Creativity: This exercise lets us practise free association.

Accessing the unconscious: The exercise should be done quickly so that there is no time to think, and the very first word that comes to mind is used.

4 **Counting Words**

Procedure: Two players improvise a scene together. Two others stand to one side, and call out a number to each player before they speak. The players are only allowed to say that many words.

Themes:

Handing over control: Here again, the players' thoughts are directed to a task – counting the words.

5 **Development of New Products**

Procedure: The task is to develop a new product or concept. Goals are set, and the exercise begins. One person brings in the first idea, and the others build on it with a series of "Yes, and . . ." (either spoken out loud or as an attitude). When the players run out of ideas, a new suggestion may be made. Only at the end may the products or concepts be evaluated.

Themes:

Accepting offers: The other team members' ideas are built upon.

Co-creativity: It is the team that develops the new products and ideas.

6 **Freeze Tag with Objects**

Procedure: Just two players come to the stage. They are given an object, for example a plastic bottle. They play a scene using the bottle, but they must never use the bottle as an actual bottle. Instead, the bottle could be a microphone, a rat, a torch, and so on. As soon as any member of the audience recognizes what the bottle is, they should shout "*Freeze.*" The players freeze, a new player comes on stage, taps one of the two on the shoulder, and that person leaves the stage. The new player then starts a new scene, with more original uses for the bottle.

Themes:

Creativity: The players must constantly see something new in the object.

Leading and allowing ourselves to be led: Everyone must be able to launch new stories with their own ideas, and also build on others' ideas.

7   Giving Presents

Procedure: This exercise requires two players. One player hands the other an imaginary object, and says, "*I brought you a present!*" In doing so, he should try to "mime" the size and weight of the gift. The other player unwraps it and replies, "*Oh, thank you, it's a . . .,*" and should try to work out what it is from the clues given by the first player.

Variant:

Again, two players. The first hands an object to the second, saying: "*Hi, I brought you a . . .*"

The other player takes it and answers "*Thanks, I can . . . with it!*"

Here is an example:

Player A: "*Hello, I brought you a hammer.*"
Player B: "*Thanks. I can build a house with it.*"

Themes:

Creativity: The players must be able to say quickly what they have received, and what they will do with it, without thinking about it for too long.

Making our partner look good: In this exercise, the players give each other gifts.

8   I am tree

Procedure: All players stand in a circle. One player moves to the centre and says, for example, "I am a tree." A second player joins her and says, for example, "I am a squirrel on the tree." A third player may then say something like, "I am a nut." Each player tries to expand the image, and there are never more than three players on stage. Then the first player takes one of the others with her, saying, "I'm taking the squirrel with me," or "I'm taking the nut with me," and those two players go back out to stand in the circle. The player left in the middle now repeats what he is, for example, "I am a nut." Two new players come in and repeat the process, thus building a new picture, and so on.

Themes:

Accepting offers: The offer on the table must always be built upon.

Teamwork: Again, only good collaboration between all players can generate meaningful and entertaining images.

9   **Making Links**

Procedure: One player stands in the centre, with two other players next to him. The two players call out a word to him, and he must try to find a link between these two words. For example, "plaster" and "looroll": "*If you scrape the plaster from the walls, you can make great looroll from it.*" The links do not have to be realistic; the idea is to foster the ability to form analogies.

Themes:

Creativity: Analogies foster creativity.

Accessing the unconscious: Here again, the unconscious partly guides the association process.

10   **Mantra**

Procedure: Two players improvise a scene together. Before the scene, each is given a mantra by the audience, for example "*I love all people,*" or "*I can do this.*" The players must repeat this silently to themselves throughout the scene.

Themes:

Handing over control: The players' task is to improvise without monitoring themselves, by concentrating entirely on the mantra.

11   **Metamorphosis**

Procedure: All players stand in a circle, and pass an object to each other. Each person must use the object in a different way. Let us say the object is a scarf: for Player A it may be a snake, and Player A passes it on to Player B as a snake. Then for Player B it may be a flying carpet, and so on.

Themes:

Creativity: The players must always be able to see something new in the object.

Accepting offers: Others' offers must always be accepted.

12   **Perspectives Game**

Procedure: A problem is introduced and briefly described. Three players then come to the front of the stage, and must take on three roles given to them by the audience. Unusual perspectives may be applied – for example, a player may demonstrate a product. All three players then take turns to present their perspective on the problem. Whenever a player begins to speak, the other two must be quiet, as it is important that all three perspectives be accorded the same amount of time.

Themes:

> **Changing perspectives:** This is a good exercise for putting ourselves in the other person's shoes, and for us to see how differently other people may perceive a situation.
>
> **Accepting offers:** Here again, the players must accept each other's offers.
>
> **Leading and allowing ourselves to be led:** When the scene has to develop from a player's own perspective, that player must take over the lead. When the scene is played from another's perspective, the players must allow themselves to be led.

13 Re-naming Objects

Procedure: The players go around the room, re-naming everything they see. For example, when they see a wall, they may say, "*Door*," or a chair may be a cow, and so on.

Themes:

> **Creativity:** This exercise is about getting into "open mode" (John Cleese), and seeing everything not only for what it is, but for what it could be.
>
> **Accessing the unconscious:** Here again, the players should say the first word that comes to mind, without thinking about it. Ideally, they should even surprise themselves.

14 Spitfire

Procedure: Two players improvise a scene. Two members of the audience can call out words at any time, which must then be incorporated into the scene.

Themes:

> **Creativity:** Players must make new connections between what is already there and the new words coming from outside.
>
> **Accessing the unconscious:** Once again, the players have to incorporate words into the scene without thinking about it, and they may surprise even themselves.

15 Take It Back

Procedure: Two players improvise a scene. Whenever a bell rings, a player must make a new offer, as in the example below:

Player A: "*I hate you!*" – Bell rings
Player A: "*I love you!*" – Bell rings again
Player A: "*I desire you!*"

At this point, the scene may continue.
Another example:

Player B: "*This is a sword.*" – Bell rings
Player B: "*This is a ring.*"

Again, at this point, the scene may continue.

Themes:

> **Creativity:** The players must constantly make new suggestions.
>
> **Accessing the unconscious:** Since the players have no time to think, they have to take the first thought that comes into their head. These thoughts often come from the unconscious.

16 Whisky Mixer

Procedure: All players stand in a circle and pass words to each other. The phrase "Whisky Mixer" is passed to the right, and the phrase "Mister Whisker" goes to the left. With the phrase "Misty Vista," a player can change the direction of the game. The most important rule is that anyone who cannot help laughing has to run once round the outside of the circle.

Themes:

> **Failing with good humour**: This game is funniest when people make mistakes.

Bibliography

Basadur, M. (1994). *Simplex: A flight to creativity*. Canada: The Creative Education Foundation.

Csíkszentmihályi, M. (1996). *Creativity: Flow and the psychology of discovery and invention*. New York: Harper Perennial.

Edmondson, A. (2013). *Teaming to innovate*. San Francisco: Bass & Wiley.

Goergens, S. F. (2009). *Brainstorming – Irren ist quantitativ*. München: Focus 05.

Haslam, A., Adarves-Yorno, I., Postmes, T., and Jans, L. (2013). The collective origins of valued originality – A social identity approach to creativity. *Personality and Social Psychology Review*, 17, 384–401.

Jackson, P. Z. (2015). *Easy – Your lifepass to creativity and confidence*. London: The Solution Focus.

Johnstone, K. (1981). *Improvisation and the theatre*. 2nd edn. London: Methuen Paperback.

Kelley, T. and Littman, J. (2001). *The art of innovation – Lessons in creativity from IDEO, America's leading design firm*. London: Bookmarque.

Koppett, K. (2001). *Training to imagine – Practical improvisational theatre techniques to enhance creativity, teamwork, leadership and learning*. Sterling: Stylus.

Kruse, O. (1997). *Kreativität als Ressource für Veränderung und Wachstum.* Tübingen: Deutsche Gesellschaft für Verhaltenstherapie.

Leonard, K. and Yorton, T. (2015). *Yes, and – Lessons from the second city.* New York: Collins.

Nachmanovitch, S. (1990). *Free play – Improvisation in life and art.* New York: Penguin Putnam.

Schwarz, G. (2003). *Konfliktmanagement.* Wiesbaden: Gabler & GWV.

Wallas, G. (1926). *The art of thought.* Kent: Solis.

Online sources

Beglinger, M. (2013). Der Staat der Physiker (Cern). *Das Magazin.* Available at: www.dasmagazin.ch/2013/10/25/der-staat-der-physiker/?reduced=true [Accessed 29 May 2018].

Knauß, F. (2013). Genies sind keine Einzelgänger. *Wirtschaftswoche.* Available at: www.wiwo.de/erfolg/trends/kreativitaet-genies-sind-keine-einzelgaenger/8946456.html [Accessed 29 May 2018].

Chapter 6

Status

Introduction

"Status" is a very central concept from improvisational theatre that can be widely applied in the domain of training and leadership. Keith Johnstone (1981), who first established the term in this context, found that scenes on stage became far more vivid and true-to-life when the actors had to consciously alter how they related to each other. For example, they might be asked to position themselves slightly above or below their partner on stage.

The term stems from Latin, and means "standing," "condition," or "position." These days, "status" is mostly used to describe the position a person occupies within the hierarchy of a society – their social status. "Status symbols" are used accordingly in an attempt to shore up or raise this social status.

There is, moreover, a certain "status behaviour," which Johnstone describes in his book "Improvisation and the Theatre" (1981), referring in this case to status as something that we "do," as opposed to social status, which is something we "have." Status behaviour always takes place when people interact, and usually subconsciously. If two people walking along the pavement are about to collide, the one who moves out of the way has the lower status at that moment. This status behaviour is very primitive, stretching right back to the earliest interactions between animals and humans.

Figure 6.1 © Evi Fill

In fact, we are constantly monitoring ourselves and others for status indicators. Body language, voice, verbal language, and how we deal with space and time all communicate the status of every one of us. However, our status is not fixed; rather, it changes constantly according to our fascinating relations to one another, as we endlessly renegotiate our status. A beggar may well radiate a status superior (high status) to the people from whom they are begging for money. In contrast, a manager can take up a status inferior (low status) to their staff. In all such cases, high and low status can only be identified in relation to other people. This means that we cannot simply "take" high status; it must also be given. No matter how many high-status signals we transmit, if others do not acknowledge our status, then the effort is wasted. On stage and screen, a person's status is chiefly communicated by the reactions of others, for example by their admiration, awe, or fear.

Status behaviour can also be used as a self-defence mechanism. High-status behaviour aims to instil respect and send the message, "*I am stronger than you; don't start with me!*" Low-status messages saying, "*I am weaker than you; it's not worth attacking me*" are an attempt to pacify the opponent.

In this chapter I will deal with the subject of status, and "attempt to answer the following questions" (low status), or "I will answer the following questions for you" (high status):

- How can I lower my status?
- How can I raise my status?
- How else can I influence status?
- How can I consciously change my status?
- How does status behaviour influence social status?
- How do I consciously establish status in my professional life?

Low status

If we are to change our own status, we must think about our body language, our voice, and our verbal language. Initially, it is best to pay conscious attention to our own status and that of others, and decide which status we prefer to take on at different times. Only then should we attempt to change our status, and then only when necessary. In the following chapters I will look in more detail at situations where it makes sense to take on low status, and which advantages low-status behaviour can have.

Low status can be communicated with the following signals:

Body language

Table 6.1 Low-status body language

Leg and foot position	Standing on one leg
	Turning our feet inwards
Head position	Holding our head slightly to one side

Posture	Making ourselves small
	Letting our shoulders hang
	Closed posture
Eyes	Looking, then quickly looking away
	Frequent blinking
Movement	Agitated and fidgety movements
Touching	Touching our own body, particularly our face

Table 6.2 Low-status voice and verbal language

Breathing	Shallow and rapid breathing
Voice	Speaking quietly
	High voice
Verbal language	A lot of "um" and "er," or other filler words
	Hesitation
	Allowing ourselves to be interrupted
	Criticizing ourselves
	Defending ourselves ("I had no other choice.")
	Using the subjunctive and related modal verbs ("I would," "I should," "I could")
	Using the passive form ("It can be done," rather than "We can do that.")
	Using a lot of adverbs that reinforce (very, thoroughly, completely …) or fill out (obviously, naturally …)

Voice and verbal language

However, none of these status signals in isolation is enough to alter our own status. What counts is our behaviour overall, our opposite number, and our own attitude.

Low status and humour

Comedians and clowns are members of a profession that makes a living almost exclusively from low status. Johnstone (1981) observed that they work according to the "see-saw" principle, whereby they lower either their own or another's status. The audience thus pays to see others have low status, but without having to feel sympathy for them. Watching television shows such as "It'll Be Alright on the Night" or "America's Funniest Home Videos" gives us a similar type of enjoyment – as long as we do not see the subsequent consequences of the mishaps, and are able to believe that everything worked out for the best. Particularly amusing is when a person with high status plummets to a low status, for example through an accident such as the "classic" slipping on a banana skin. In contrast, we would find it not at all funny if a person of already low status, such as a frail old man, were to slip and fall.

High status

High status can be communicated by the following behaviour:

Body language

Table 6.3 High-status body language

Leg and foot position	Standing on both feet Feet placed approximately shoulder width apart
Head position	Head is held straight The head hardly moves
Posture	Making ourselves big Erect and open posture
Eyes	Maintaining eye contact Eyes move little
Movement	Calm and intentional movements Large, expansive gestures
Touching	Touching others

Voice and verbal language

Table 6.4 High-status voice and verbal language

Breathing	Calm and regular breathing
Voice	Speaking loudly and clearly Deep voice
Verbal language	Speaking in whole sentences Adding pauses Commenting Storytelling Name-dropping (for example, "Barack and I ...") Asking questions Interrupting others Judging others – criticizing or praising! (Even by praising others we position ourselves above them, thus raising our own status.) Avoiding the subjunctive and vague formulations (instead: "I will," "I want," "I can") Using the active form ("We can do that," or even better, "I can do that")

Politicians tend to be masters of the high-status game, and are specifically coached for it. For example, they learn that by offering their hand for a handshake with the back of the hand facing upwards, they are assuming a position of higher status. They then round this out by touching the other person on the shoulder. The other may, in turn, offset this by doing the same. This makes for the ideal, classic photo of politicians.

Figure 6.2 © Evi Fill

Politicians in particular are forever using touch to raise their own status: by touching others, we raise our own status.

Another example of high-status behaviour from a politician is the way in which the newly elected United States president, Donald Trump, on meeting the United Kingdom prime minister, Theresa May, for the first time in January 2017, consistently called her "Theresa," while she called him "Mr President."

Dimensions of status: space, size, age

Status and space

In their book *Jenseits der Hierarchie – Status im beruflichen Alltag aktiv gestalten* (*Beyond Hierarchy – Actively Managing Status in the Workplace*) (2015), Professors Johannes Lehner and Walter Ötsch of the University of Linz show that status always relates to territory. This involves defending or conquering a domain or area. By occupying extensive territory and taking large spaces for ourselves, we award ourselves higher status. Battles over status often involve territorial claims.

People who frequently like to take on high status, known as "high-status players," even occupy a lot of space with their bodies and movements. They stand straight and firm, make large gestures, push into others' personal space, and touch their opposite numbers.

We extend our space, and thus our status, by marking out our territory: by placing our towel on a sunbed at the beach, a photo of our family on the desk in our office, or our jacket on the back of our chair. Even just by leaning on an object, we are taking possession of it. Such territory marking is a standard signal of status. Having a larger office, a larger company car, or a parking spot near the entrance are all examples of the daily business of fighting for territory within an organization. Changes to these territorial rights will often lead to conflicts of status and power. Lehner and Ötsch (2015) state that clearly defined territory can help us avoid conflicts, and strengthen our bond to the organization, whereas open areas with unclear separation of space encourage conflict. In a time of open-plan offices without clearly assigned workspaces, this is a hot topic!

Not only people, but also spaces and buildings or objects can possess status. For example, taller buildings or rooms with high ceilings have a higher status. This is why there is constant competition to have the tallest building in the city, or better still in the world. Government buildings and churches were and are built to radiate higher status, and thus force observers or visitors into a kind of low status. However, the status of a place also depends on who is entering it: the boss's office may not have a particular feeling of status for the boss themselves, but it will for another staff member, even if the boss is not present. A well-loved status game, then, is to make the most of the boss's absence by sitting in their chair or, even better, putting our feet up on their desk. This is fun, because we can lower the boss's status without having to fear the consequences. As long as no one walks in on us . . .

Status and height

Taller people are at an advantage in status games. It is easier for them to assume a higher status, if only because others are forced to look up to them. But height alone does not confer high status; it must be backed up by the appropriate body language. In fact, taller people will often make themselves smaller, thus lowering their own status.

Status and age

Status is also linked to age. For a younger person, with as yet little experience, it is more difficult (but not impossible!) to assume a high status. It becomes easier with age, and others will also tend to confer a higher status on us as we become older. However, with more advanced years, our status will fall again. As we retire from professional life, our social status falls, and when we become slower and frailer it becomes increasingly difficult for us to maintain high-status behaviour.

Status flexibility

Imagine the following three managers . . .

Manager A: The staff like A as a person, and appreciate his friendly manner. However, A has difficulty imposing his will, as his staff find ways to continue working as they always have before. They also have no difficulty in diverting A from his chosen path.

Manager B: The staff respect B for his professional competence, but B is unapproachable and unpredictable. Nobody would ever risk criticizing B, or openly questioning his opinion.

Manager C: People say that as a boss, C works "on an equal footing" with his staff, but is also able to garner respect. He pushes his staff, but is always ready to give support when needed. C follows through on his decisions, and is prepared to receive honest feedback from his staff and make joint decisions with them.

These three managers most probably differ in their status behaviour. It is likely that manager A sends out many low-status signals, and thus has no chance of garnering respect from his staff. Manager B doubtless transmits almost exclusively at the high-status "frequency," and is probably more feared than appreciated by his staff. Manager C is best at altering his status according to the circumstances. He puts himself in his colleagues' shoes and adapts his status to the needs of the situation, but still manages to gather personal esteem when results are needed. Thus, we see that leadership is not only about leadership style, but also status behaviour.

This is all about **status flexibility**! It is important to be able to read other people's status signals and adapt our own status to the situation at hand. Most people prefer a certain status level, without being aware of it. However, everyone is able to modify their status within a certain range. In my seminars, we look at how to broaden this range and thus increase our status flexibility. This status flexibility is vital to successful communication and interaction; for example, in a job interview it is useful to lower our status slightly below that of the head of personnel.

A first step towards status flexibility is to develop an awareness for our own and others' status.

The following exercise can help:

Exercise

Status parties

All players are given a number that is visible to everyone else, but not to that player, for example on a sticker. Each player can see everyone else's number, but not their own. There are always a few more numbers than players, so that players cannot guess numbers by a process of elimination. Thus, for 10 players there may be 14 numbers. The lowest number represents the lowest status, and the highest number represents the highest status.

Then the party can get started. First, it is established that a certain firm is holding a celebration for a certain reason. Each player's number represents their status, and initially nobody knows their own status. Each player has to interact with all the other players according to their status (number). Everyone remains on their feet, and they mingle and talk with each other.

At the end, all players line up in what they believe to be their order of status. People outside the game may not help. Then everyone gets to look at their own numbers to see who is standing in the right or wrong positions, and they discuss how they felt in their roles.

A high status has a different effect than a low status. Raising our own status gives us more authority and assertiveness. Lowering our own status, and in doing so raising the status of others, communicates empathy. Both techniques are appropriate in different situations.

High and low status thus have advantages and disadvantages:

Advantages of high status

- greater assertiveness
- greater authority
- greater credibility
- others will listen and take us seriously

Disadvantages of high status

- more competitive behaviour in others
- others have less space
- high-status behaviour makes others feel insecure, and lowers their status

Advantages of low status

- we give space to others
- we acknowledge others' status
- we often come across as having more empathy and being more pleasant

Disadvantages of low status

- less assertiveness
- less authority
- less credibility
- others will take less notice of us

Inner and outer status

Status has a lot to do with our own self-confidence. And when our own (internal) attitude is out of sync with our (external) status, it shows through very quickly on the outside. For example, we may send out high-status signals to cover up our own insecurity. Status flexibility always requires self-confidence; it takes courage to take space for ourselves, and also to give space to others.

However, this does not mean that those who feel insecure are excluded from experimenting with their own status. The expression "Fake it till you make it," and a certain method of acting both imply taking on a character from outside and acquiring that character inside. It involves observing others, observing ourselves, and trying out small changes (for example, standing squarely on both feet), and seeing what effect such changes have.

Ways of changing status

We can change status either by raising or lowering our own status, or by raising or lowering that of others. We thus have four possibilities:

1 We can raise our own status, for example by telling our own success stories.
2 We can raise our own status by lowering others' status, for example by criticizing them.
3 We can lower our own status, for example through self-criticism.
4 We can lower our own status by raising others' status, for example by expressing appreciation or admiration for them.

Status can also be changed in the following ways: (adapted and expanded from http://improwiki.com/de/wiki/improtheater/status, accessed 29 May 2018)

Changing status through benevolence

Table 6.5 Ways of changing status

	Changing our own status	Changing others' status
High status	Not accepting help	Helping others, protecting others
Low status	Needing and accepting help	Asking for help from others

Changing status through praise/criticism

Table 6.6 Ways of changing status

	Changing our own status	Changing others' status
High status	Praising ourselves, telling our own success stories	Criticizing or praising others
Low status	Self-deprecation, self-criticism	Honouring or admiring others

Changing status by occupying space

Table 6.7 Ways of changing status

	Changing our own status	*Changing others' status*
High status	Sweeping gestures, pacing around over a wide area, occupying a lot of space	Pushing others to one side, leaving them little space
Low status	Taking little space for ourselves	Giving others a lot of space, deferring to them

Changing status through height/posture

Table 6.8 Ways of changing status

	Changing our own status	*Changing others' status*
High status	Standing up, using a straight posture, making ourselves bigger	Looking down on others
Low status	Remaining seated, kneeling, making ourselves smaller	"Bowing down" before others

Changing status through proximity

Table 6.9 Ways of changing status

	Changing our own status	*Changing others' status*
High status	Coming close to others	Touching others
Low status	Enduring others coming close and touching us	Avoiding others

Changing status by switching to the meta level

Another way of raising our own status is by switching to the meta level. This involves observing proceedings "from above," then commenting on what we observe. This can be done, for example, by reflecting on processes in team meetings:

> *We're already way off-subject.*
> *I'm detecting sub-textual conflicts here. Can we talk about them openly?*

This method may also be applied when others take on a very high status, and it is difficult for us to raise our own status by changing our status behaviour. Here are two examples:

> *I've noticed that I'm always being interrupted when I'm speaking. Why is that?*
> *I see that you're not taking what I say seriously. What's that about?*

Observing processes at the meta level like this automatically raises our own status.

"Happy high status"

In my training sessions, when I ask participants to improvise scenes depicting or deploying high status, their initial impulse is often to make themselves bigger at the cost of their counterparts. They copy status behaviour that they recognize from their daily lives, and take space for themselves by reducing their counterparts' space, or they raise their own status by lowering others' status. This is certainly one way to occupy high status. However, it is usually perceived as arrogant, unpleasant, or aloof.

But there is another route to high status: "happy high status." This type of high status is positive, self-confident throughout, and does not rely on lowering the status of others. Happy high status can be achieved as follows:

> Colleague: "*I don't yet understand this task. Could you help me?*"
> Manager: "*I'm happy to give you some time this afternoon. Please come back at 14:00.*"

The manager is clearly in control of this encounter. She does not let herself simply be monopolized, but is nonetheless ready to help.

Here is the same situation without positive high status:

> Colleague: "*I don't yet understand this task. Could you help me?*"
> Manager: "*I hired you specifically for this task. You'll have to sort it out yourself!*"

Here, the status is still high ("I don't have time") but is now disparaging ("You'll have to sort it out yourself").

However, even happy high status requires status flexibility, as it is not useful to cling onto it irrespective of the circumstances. We should always adapt our own status according to the situation!

Status and conflicts

In most conflict situations, safeguarding our own status is rarely bottom of the list. This is why status and conflicts are closely linked. If both opponents have low status, conflict will rarely occur at all, as both sides will tend to avoid it. If both opponents have high status and one lowers their own, conflict is avoided as the high-status player can impose their own agenda. If both sides start off with high status but are both prepared to lower their own status, a compromise can be found.

But if both opponents hold onto their high status, then the conflict will escalate. If neither side will back down by lowering their own status, then the conflict may be severe. Only if both are prepared to raise and lower their status during the conflict – that is, to demonstrate status flexibility – will a consensus be reached.

Status and women

Concerning women, many high-status signals such as standing or sitting with legs apart are seen as inappropriate or even indecent. Compared to men, there is a far greater expectation for women to occupy less space, avoid interrupting others, stay out of the spotlight, and so on. It is therefore more difficult for women to find a high status that on the one hand suits them as an individual, and on the other hand – and this is key – is acceptable to others.

When flirting, it is still typical for women to assume low status by touching their hair or face, holding their head a little to one side, and gazing upwards from a low position. In the past, women were brought up to display low-status behaviour, and even today, changes to our society and to women's bearing are still rather slow to be seen.

Figure 6.3 © Evi Fill

Occupying low status makes it easier to come across as agreeable, to make friends and to be liked. This may be why some leaders find that it is lonely at the top. For many women, close relationships seem to be more important than they are for men, to the extent that women will prioritize relationships over their career ambitions. Women also often say they have an uneasy relationship with power. In my seminars, when I ask women if they want power, they usually say no. When asked the same question, men will often say yes straight away, and express that they perceive power to be something positive.

Status behaviour and social status

Matthew effect

Lehner and Ötsch (2015) describe the connection between status behaviour and social status (that is, the value or significance of a person in the eyes of the public, which then accords them a specific place in the social hierarchy). A person with higher social status can more easily impose their will, impress others, and dominate status games. Lehner and Ötsch describe this as the "*Matthäus-Effekt*" (in English the Matthew effect, from the Holy Bible, Matthew 13:12, "to him who has will more be given, and he will have abundance; but from him who has not, even what he has will be taken away.") A high-status individual will usually be granted more recognition for the same performance as someone with lower status.

Nonetheless, social status must still be underscored by appropriate status behaviour if it is to be maintained. For example, a manager is granted official privileges and other trappings by his organization; but if he is not always able to implement what he wants in daily business, over time he will lose the respect of his colleagues. This does not mean that a manager must always occupy the high ground, but he must be capable of taking high status for himself when the situation demands it.

Hierarchy paradox

The "classic" hierarchy with clearly defined higher and lower positions is increasingly falling out of favour, either being done away with altogether, or converted into flatter hierarchies. This has the paradoxical effect of increasing the prevalence of status games (Lehner and Ötsch, 2015). Traditional hierarchies have the advantage that status need not be constantly renegotiated, as it is officially maintained by clear positions and fixed rules of behaviour. Once someone has reached a certain position it is almost impossible to knock them from their perch, even if they prove to be unsuitable for that position (which is at the same time a major disadvantage to such a system).

However, when traditional hierarchies are dissolved or modified, as is happening today, questions of power and influence do not simply evaporate. They are merely asked and answered differently. Since officially granted functions or positions now offer far less orientation and stability, if any at all, they must now be secured through status games, and defended against competition.

Status behaviour in professional life

Status for managers

Managers always find themselves in a kind of "sandwich." They lead their staff, and have their own leaders above them (business owners, the market, or in the Pope's case, "God" – there is always someone or something higher than us). This means that most managers in an organization must assume a slightly lower status than those above, and a slightly higher status than those below. This is not to be confused with "crawling to the bigwigs and bullying the underlings"; as shown earlier, we can raise our own status without looking down on others, and lower our own status without becoming subservient. The advantage of doing so is that endless battles for status can be avoided.

There are other good reasons for managers to adapt their status. For example, if they need to appear convincing or to implement decisions, then higher status will help a great deal. But if true teamwork is required, and everybody needs to be brought in – such as when resolving complex situations or in creative processes – then a lower status can be useful. Only then will other team members have the space to open up and feel free to express their opinions and offer feedback. If innovation, creativity, and synergy are wanted or required, positions of too high a status tend to foster inhibition.

Picture the following situation: a manager is leaning right back in his huge office chair, well back from his desk, his legs casually crossed, and his arms folded behind his head. He says to his staff member (who is sitting on a normal office chair), "*Mr X, I'd like honest feedback from you! Tell me, what do you think of me?!*" How likely is the staff member to feel that this is a genuine request for open and honest feedback?

Figure 6.4 © Evi Fill

For comparison, here is another situation: the manager and his colleague are sitting at a round table, both on similar chairs. The manager's legs are parallel to each other, and his body is slightly inclined towards his counterpart. His arms are resting on the table. He says to his colleague, "*Mr X, I'd very much like to hear from you how you feel about my work as your manager.*"

Figure 6.5 © Evi Fill

When the status differential is too great, staff do not believe that managers can put themselves in their position, and they feel insecure. This then leads to managers receiving less information and less straight feedback.

This exercise can help us learn how to increase our own status flexibility:

Exercise

Status see-saw

Two players improvise a scene together, whereby at the start there is a clear status gradient. For the first scene I usually take a job interview, with an exaggerated status gradient. At the start of the scene, the head of personnel's status should be as high as possible, and the interviewee should assume as low a status as possible (the more extreme, the better). On a scale of 1–10 (with 1 representing very low status and 10 representing very high status), the interviewer should be a 10, the interviewee a 1.

Once the interview is under way, the players can start to "see-saw" their status, slowly changing their relative status levels. The interviewer lowers her status, as the interviewee slowly raises his. By the end, the head of personnel should have a very low status (1), and the interviewee a very high status (10). Usually, the interviewer finishes by pleading with the interviewee to take the job. For the see-saw to work, a reason is needed, and the players have to come up with a reason on the spot. Examples are that the interviewee is the son of the company's owner, but doesn't come out with it until later, or the interviewer falls in love with the interviewee, and so on.

In periods of great change, it is particularly important for leaders to know that resistance often arises because people's status is under threat. Indeed, restructuring frequently negatively impacts the status of those it affects, through loss either of utility, of tasks, of responsibilities – or even of the job itself. Those who announce change enjoy enhanced status; those who are subject to change see their status fall. Transparency, open communication, and speaking face-to-face with those affected are ways to minimize the almost unavoidable loss of status for staff.

Status for trainers

Of course, trainers also need to adapt their status to the situation at hand. As they stand before a group and wish to communicate their subject matter convincingly and with credibility, a somewhat higher status is certainly appropriate. However, when it is the participants who take centre stage – during exercises, role-play, group work, or discussions – then the trainer needs to lower their own status, to place the focus on the participants and make it easier for them to concentrate on their own status.

I once attended one of Keith Johnstone's workshops. He was fairly old already, but nevertheless would sometimes lie down on the floor while teaching. This was clearly a technique to lower his status as a "great master" in the eyes of his participants, and thus to create as much space and security as possible for their learning.

Status for salespeople

Status is critical in sales. On the one hand, the salesperson must be convincing and appear self-confident; on the other hand, they need to place the client at the centre and make them feel comfortable.

Here is an exercise I use with salespeople:

Exercise

Status sale

Four players improvise a scene together. For example, one of them is sell-ing a valuable personal item (a classic car, an antique piano, and so on). Each player has a number whispered in their ear (1 for the lowest status, 4 for the highest), which they then have to apply in the scene. Players only know their own numbers. They come on stage one by one to look at the item for sale. At the end, the seller decides to whom they will sell their item. The audience is then invited to guess which player received which number.

After this exercise, it can be discussed why a certain person was chosen as the buyer. It is usually someone whose number was below the seller's status. The same principle applies here as in a job interview: lowering our own status slightly below that of the customer, and thus raising theirs.

A seller should, therefore, take on a slightly lower status than the customer, but a high status when it comes to the product: the seller is the expert regarding the product, but the customer is the expert regarding their own needs and wishes, and the salesperson needs to satisfy these.

Conclusion

Status behaviour can be changed, to some extent irrespective of a person's social status and finances. The key to success is increasing our status flexibility so that we can adapt our status to the situation at hand.

Here is a summary of the main points about status:

- Status is "always and everywhere"
- Status behaviour is largely subconscious – and a taboo subject
- Status relates to territory
- Status exists in relation to others
- Status can be changed
- Low status enables honest feedback
- Low status opens up space for others

- High status is not better than low status
- High status facilitates implementing our own wishes
- High status can be achieved without devaluing others
- High status is harder to achieve for women
- Status flexibility is supported by self-confidence
- Status flexibility can resolve conflicts
- Status flexibility is key to successful communication and leadership

I hope you now feel like experimenting with your status behaviour and broadening your capabilities. Ideally, you should start by observing yourself and others. A good exercise is to judge other people's status relative to each other, for example in a café, at the bus stop, or in the canteen. Note who has the highest status, and who has the lowest, and if this changes as you watch. This is a very entertaining learning opportunity!

Practical examples

Status workshop for Aeon Consulting Group

Key points

- *Company:*
  Aeon Consulting Group is a consultancy headquartered in Austria. It operates at an international level.

- *Assignment:*
  Workshop on presentation ability, natural authority, and status

- *Duration:*
  2 x 1 day

- *Target group:*
  All staff at the company

- *Objectives:*
  Participants aimed to . . .

  - professionalize their bearing, their presence, and how they appear to groups

---

- get to know their own body language and how to use it more consciously
- learn more about their own status when communicating with other people, and learn to alter it as necessary
- expand their room for manoeuvre in unexpected situations
- maintain better control when dealing with "difficult" customers
- improve their abilities to improvise, and their assertiveness
- use the group experience to draw closer together as a team

Starting point and highlights

In 2011, the two heads of Aeon Consulting Group contacted me to request a team development workshop using methods from improv theatre. This first workshop concentrated on the foundations of improvisation and teamwork. In 2014, a second workshop took place, this time focusing on the themes of personal presentation, natural authority, and status. As project managers and consultants, the staff of Aeon Consulting Group spend much of their time with customers; status flexibility is thus part of daily business for them. Therefore, "status" was the focus of the workshop.

One of the exercises was as follows:

Exercise

Status challenges

Two players are given a situation by the audience. For example, they have to be two colleagues at a conference, or two politicians at an event. They then improvise the scene while both fighting for the highest status. From time to time, the players must "freeze," and the audience is asked which player has the highest status at that point, and why.

A variant to this is that both players should fight to have the lowest status.

This exercise helps the players learn how to raise or lower their status, and the audience learns from seeing them do this.

We also used the "King and Servant" game:

Exercise

The king game

A volunteer plays the king and sits on a "throne" on the stage. The king is effectively the customer. The players have to come on stage one by one and do something to interest the king (customer). When the king gets bored, he snaps his fingers and the next "servant" comes on. Each servant aims to hold the king's attention for as long as possible.

Many improv theatre exercises involve immediate feedback. In this case, the feedback is provided by the king snapping his fingers. After the status exercises, it was important to reflect on how vital it is to adapt and change status in customer meetings.

Customer feedback from Ute Langthaler and Erich Wlasak (CEOs):

We booked the workshops because we wanted to work on our ability to communicate with more than just words, and also because one of our board members had experience with improv theatre. As board members, at first we were unsure of exactly what benefits we could expect, so we went in with very open minds. The days we spent together actually helped us in several ways, not least because as participants we learned how to come closer together in a very refreshing and energizing way. In these workshops, laughing together and learning together were not self-contradictory.

What memories and impressions have we taken away from the improv theatre workshop? To experiment, within a safe environment, with how we can deal with different situations, and how we can push the envelope. We also very much appreciated the chance to work on our communicative abilities through entertaining exercises, and without having to listen to a lot of theory.

We have fond memories of the good time we had, and the following aspects:

- a deeper understanding of how to work with our own status
- a better sense of how communication can flow, and what can crop up to block it
- encouragement to believe in our own creativity and spontaneity

Offboarding workshop for Swisscom

Key points

- *Company:*
  Swisscom AG is a leading Swiss telecommunications company.

- *Assignment:*
  Offboarding workshop for a team, using applied improvisation

- *Duration:*
  Work with applied improvisation: ½ day

- *Target group:*
  Managers

- *Objectives:*
  Participants aimed to . . .

    - look back on what they had achieved together
    - take their leave of the team in its current form
    - get to know their own body language and how to use it more consciously
    - learn more about status, and learn how to alter it as necessary

---

Starting point and highlights

As part of a restructuring process, a management team of Swisscom AG was being dissolved. To give them a chance to take leave of one another and from the work they had done together, offboarding events were organized. One of these was a half-day workshop using methods from improv theatre. Since this team would no longer exist in its current form, I chose to open the workshop with a look back at what they had achieved together, in the form of stories. Each participant was to tell a story from their time together as a team; the story was to be one that evoked happy memories and that meant a lot to the storyteller. The aim of telling the stories was to enable the participants to think once more about the successes of the team, and focus on the positive; this would help them concentrate on their individual future careers.

Given that this workshop was not about continuing teamwork, I also focused on the subject of status, as every individual can benefit from increased status flexibility, for example in internal or external job interviews, or as the manager of a new team.

One exercise on this subject was the "Status See-saw":

Exercise

Status see-saw

Two players improvise a scene together, with a significant status gradient at the start. On a scale of 1–10, Person A takes on a very low status (1), and Person B takes on a very high status (10). The situation changes gradually, so that by the end the status gradient has completely reversed, so that Person A has a very high status (10), and Person B has a very low status (1).

This exercise is excellent for preparing for job interviews. As already mentioned, it is helpful for an interviewee to be able to lower their status slightly below that of the head of personnel.

Feedback from several participants:

I found this workshop, or rather the theme, quite "daring," especially in this difficult period. In the end, though, the theme was not too daring; rather, it was most fascinating. We were guided with care and respect, and we all joined in, even though we were a little uneasy at the start. I would summarize the workshop like this: a success, different, creative, thinking big, playful style, we all laughed a lot and I myself gained a lot from it. I would recommend it to others.

The chance to experiment meant that the participants could feel what happens (energy, others' reaction) within themselves or within a group/team.

I got a lot from this workshop, particularly concerning status and roles. I sometimes smile to myself when I see people not behaving appropriately for their role. It has stayed with me, for sure. I was also impressed by the methods used concerning communication. I've already applied these methods where communication was difficult, and we all ended up laughing together. To sum up, I gained a lot, and will certainly make more use of this sort of subject matter!

Something that has stayed with me from the workshop is the subject of our personal demeanour and the effect it has on others. Since we talked about it intensively, I can see it much more in other people. It's really fascinating to see how people behave, for example when people at different levels of hierarchy are together in a room. That's what left the deepest impression on me.

Exercises on status

1 **Scenes in a Lift**

    Procedure: Two volunteers come to the front. One is the boss, while the other is a staff member. The boss has just fired the staff member because he made a big mistake. The players have to wait for the lift, and both get in the lift when it comes. Apart from a brief greeting, they must say nothing to each other. At the end, the audience comments on the players' body language, whereby the boss has high status, and the staff member low status.

    Themes:

    Status sensitivity: This exercise acts as an introduction to the subject of status. The players exhibit classic high- and low-status behaviours, without even knowing much about the subject.

    Body language: The players use the feedback to learn more about their own body language.

2 **Status Challenges**

    Procedure: Two players are given a situation by the audience. For example, they have to be two colleagues at a conference, or two politicians at an event. They then improvise the scene while both fighting for the highest status. From time to time, the players must "freeze," and the audience is asked which player has the highest status at that point, and why.

    A variant to this is that both players should fight to have the lowest status.

    Themes:

    Status flexibility: The status must be raised as high or dropped as low as possible.

    Status sensitivity: The audience gives feedback as to who has the highest or lowest status, and why.

3 **Status Circle**

    Procedure: All players stand in a circle. In the first round, they must lower the status of the player to their right. In the second round, they must raise it.

    Themes:

    Status flexibility: The players learn to alter their own and others' status.

4 **Status Demo**

    Procedure: All players improvise a party or celebration at work. Half of the players must exhibit high-status behaviour (speaking in full sentences, making and maintaining eye contact), and the other half must exhibit low-status behaviour (stuttering, looking at the floor). After a while, the players change roles. At the end, the players are asked how they felt, and what changed in them.

    Themes:

    Status sensitivity: The players become aware of high- and low-status signals, and how these signals affect their own and others' behaviour.

5 Status Feedback

Procedure: A player comes on stage and tries to stand as "neutrally" as possible. Members of the audience call out a number from 1 to 10 according to what level of status they perceive in the player on stage. If desired, feedback may also be given as to how these evaluations were arrived at, that is, which signals and body language had the effect of raising or lowering the player's status.

Themes:

> **Status sensitivity:** This exercise helps us become aware of our own status.

6 Status in Presentations

Procedure: One player comes on stage, and a number from 1 to 10 is whispered in her ear (1 is the lowest status, 10 the highest). The player must then come to the centre of the stage and announce, "*Good evening, ladies and gentlemen,*" using the status level she has been given. The audience must then guess which number she was given.

Themes:

> **Status sensitivity:** This exercise helps us recognize high- and low-status signals.

> **Status flexibility:** The obligation to adapt to the number given teaches us how to consciously change our status.

7 Status Parties

Procedure: All players are given a number that is visible to everyone else, but not to that player, for example on a sticker. The sticker is placed on the clothing. Each player can see everyone else's number, but not their own. There are always a few more numbers than players, so that players cannot guess numbers by a process of elimination. Thus, for 10 players there may be 14 numbers; for 15 players, 20 numbers. The lowest number represents the lowest status, and the highest number represents the highest status.

Then the party can get started. First, it is established that a certain firm is holding a celebration for a certain reason. Each player's number represents their status, and initially nobody knows their own status. Each player has to interact with all the other players according to their status (number). Everyone remains on their feet, and they mingle and talk with each other. With time, everyone will start to get a feeling for their own status, and can begin to act accordingly.

At the end, all players line up in what they believe to be their order of status. People outside the game may not help. Then everyone gets to look at their own numbers to see who is standing in the right or wrong positions, and they discuss how they felt in their roles.

Themes:

> **Status sensitivity:** The players learn about status in daily communication, and how it feels to take on unfamiliar roles (e.g. a manager may be given a low number, or vice versa.)

> **Status flexibility:** The players must adapt their own status to their own number and to others' numbers.

8   **Status See-saw**

Procedure: Two players improvise a scene together, for example a job interview, whereby at the start there is a clear status gradient. At the start of
the scene, the status of Player A (head of personnel) should be very high,
and Player B (the interviewee) should assume a very low status. Once the
interview is under way, the players start to "see-saw" their status, slowly
changing their relative status levels. Player A lowers her status, as Player
B slowly raises his. By the end, the head of personnel should have a very
low status, and the interviewee a very high status.

Themes:

Status sensitivity: This scene will always show clearly how status is
always an interplay between the participants. If Player A does not
lower her status, it becomes very difficult for Player B to achieve
high status.

Status flexibility: The players must be able to slowly raise or lower their
status.

9   **Status Sale**

Procedure: Four players improvise a scene together. For example, one of
them is looking for a new tenant, or is selling a valuable personal item.
Each player has a number whispered in their ear (1 for the lowest status,
4 for the highest), which they then have to apply in the scene. Players
only know their own numbers. They come on stage one by one to visit the
house or look at the item for sale. At the end, the landlord decides who will
get the room, or the seller decides to whom they will sell their item. The
audience is then invited to guess which player received which number.
After this exercise, it can be discussed why a certain person was chosen
as the tenant/buyer. It is usually someone whose number was below the
landlord's/seller's status.

Themes:

Status sensitivity: This exercise shows how status can influence situations where people are applying for something or negotiating a
sale.

Status flexibility: The middle players with a 2 or a 3 must assume a
status above or below the players with a 1 or a 4. Those with a 1 or a
4 can practise very low or high status.

10   **The King Game**

Procedure: A volunteer plays the king and sits on a "throne" on the stage. The
king is effectively the customer. The players have to come on stage one by
one and do something to interest the king (customer). When the king gets
bored, he snaps his fingers and the next "servant" comes on. Each servant
aims to hold the king's attention for as long as possible.

Themes:

Presentation: The players must convince the king of their worth in a
short time.

Building tension: They learn how to maintain interest for an extended
time.

Bibliography

Johnstone, K. (1981). *Improvisation and the theatre*. 2nd edn. London: Methuen Paperback.
Lehner, J. M. and Ötsch, W. O. (2015). *Jenseits der Hierarchie – Status im beruflichen Alltag aktiv gestalten*. 2nd edn. Weinheim: Wiley-VCH.

Online source

Boyke, G. (2015). Status. *Improwiki*. Available at: http://improwiki.com/de/wiki/improtheater/status [Accessed 29 May 2018].

Chapter 7

Storytelling

Introduction to storytelling

Before the invention of writing, stories were an essential means of passing on and preserving tradition, culture, and ancient wisdom. They were used to impart experience to others, and to convey values and standards, sometimes assisted by pictures, such as cave paintings. Without the ability to pass on our collective wisdom through relating tales and stories, this wisdom would never have spread, and other people could never have built further upon it.

Figure 7.1 © Evi Fill

Despite the invention of writing, and despite the spread of today's new forms of media, telling stories remains deeply woven into our daily lives. The field of narrative psychology goes as far as to claim that humans conceptualize and form their entire lives and environments in the form of stories. Experiences from the past are linked with the present and projected into the future, and are thus formulated into an integrated story for the person themselves and for anyone listening to them.

The American cognitive scientist Roger C. Schank (2000) believes that the ability to identify a relevant experience from the past that can help deal with a new situation is the core of intelligent behaviour. In this way, stories reduce complexity and allow us to link new knowledge with our own experiences, which makes stories an important tool for teaching and learning.

Stories can trigger emotions, thus acting as a kind of "learning turbo," as the brain researcher Manfred Spitzer (2002) put it. He stated that the registration of information in our long-term memory depends on how significant the brain's limbic system deems that information to be. A key element is a combination of the ability to remember something and the strength of the emotions that are awakened by that memory.

In the 1980s, psychologist Jérôme Bruner investigated two different approaches to reality: "logical-scientific" or "argumentative" thinking, and "narrative" thinking. Argumentative thinking gathers facts, rules, and laws about the world. It is based on data or theories, and tends towards abstraction. It concentrates on details and individual aspects of things; it establishes connections between facts and other facts, in order to generate new facts. Narrative thinking, in contrast, deals with actual or possible events, and attempts to make them concrete. It links together facts, emotions, environmental aspects, attitudes, and behaviours, and opens up possibilities. Narrative thinking creates meaning, orientation, and vision for the future. Each of these types of thinking offers a different view of the world, and both are equally important.

Stories are a trend right now, and are even important for winning elections – which themselves show a trend – in particular in the United States. The story is usually that of the hero who made his way up in the world, such as Barack Obama – from an "ordinary" black man to the President of the United States – or Donald Trump, from "mere" millionaire to multibillionaire. Part of their technique, of course, is to suggest that the common people are also heroes of the story – from Obama's "Yes we can" slogan, with its message of working together to solve the major global political issues such as justice, affluence, and world peace – to Trump's "Make America great again," with its promise of a return to America's glory days.

Stories can be used in many ways, and naturally are open to abuse. They can pass on wisdom, they can teach, and they can entertain; but they can also be used to manipulate entire societies by spreading lies in the form of "alternative facts."

Indeed, stories are always partly created by the storyteller, and even when they are entirely "true," they still follow and adapt to the subjective feelings and sensibilities of both storyteller and listener. We only have to think about stories of success and failure within any company, where any attempt to reconstruct how things "truly" happened is generally doomed. This shows that facts themselves are not the driver, but rather the goals and reasons for which a success story – or horror story – is taken up. Whatever the case, storytellers must take great care, as stories can be dangerously effective.

Many books on the subject of storytelling describe how important and effective it is to make use of stories, but rarely will they talk about how stories are actually compiled. Improvisational theatre offers a rich source of experiences, as it requires stories to be made up through teamwork on the spur of the moment. This chapter looks more closely at storytelling, and how stories can be deployed in training, team development, and presentations.

The chapter looks at the following questions:

- Where is storytelling used?
- How are stories created?
- How does improvisational theatre use collaboration to build up joint stories?
- How can companies work with stories?
- How can storytelling help teambuilding?
- How can I use storytelling in presentations?

Ways of using storytelling

Storytelling has grown beyond a way of providing amusement and imparting knowledge. It has become a method by which explicit and implicit knowledge can be passed on in the form of metaphors. The storytelling method is applied in various fields, such as in businesses, in advertising, or in psychotherapy. Insights and experiences are carried in the form of stories that speak to listeners in their individual "worlds"; listeners can then directly build them into their own range of experience.

Storytelling is also beneficial in the following ways:

- More of the brain is activated than when dealing with plain information.
- Stories give meaning and significance to facts and circumstances.
- Storytelling invites the listener or reader to bring in their own thoughts and feelings.
- Personal connections and common opinions are reinforced.
- Stories have an element of entertainment, and are passed on more often than pure facts.

Since science has started looking more closely at storytelling, and since increasing attention is being given to it, storytelling is being deployed in a growing variety of fields.

Storytelling in psychotherapy

Narrative psychology is a methodical approach to understanding how people use stories and tales to interpret and give meaning to the world. An assumption is made that people's life stories inform how they behave, how they feel, and what meaning they give to their lives. The conversation between therapist and client is seen as a joint narrative process, whereby the client relates her stories and how she approaches problems, and the therapist tells stories that contain new potential solutions. The aim of this exchange is to develop new stories together that expand the client's options.

Hypnotherapy is another area in which therapeutic messages are communicated via stories. The client is placed in a trance, so that the relevant message can be sent directly to the unconscious – bypassing conscious thought – in the form of metaphors or analogies aimed at bringing about therapeutic changes.

As already described in "Introduction to improvisational theatre," J. L. Moreno's **psychodrama** also works with stories and theatrical methods, using role-play to develop and adapt stories as a joint process.

Storytelling in companies

A well-known method for companies is called "**learning history**." This was developed in the middle of the 1990s in the United States, with employees being asked about specific occurrences within their organizations. The idea is to bring in as many different perspectives as possible (e.g. customers, employees, managers, board members). The results are then assembled and documented as a story of people's experiences. For example, at the conclusion of a change process, staff members may be asked to give their feedback in the form of stories. The "Learning History" then represents the experiences of those involved in the change process, allowing a clear picture of people's perceptions to be built up.

Another form is the **storytelling analysis**. This approach was developed in Germany at the end of the 1990s by the literary theorists Karolina Frenzel et al. (2004). It involves using employees' stories together with information on company culture and communication within the organization, with the aim of opening up new possibilities for development.

Storytelling is also used by companies in **conflict management**, enabling the involved parties' hidden attitudes and perspectives to be brought "to the table," thus allowing them to be examined as possible key elements in the conflict.

Finally, storytelling is used to make **presentations** lively and vivid. This is extremely effective, as the audience will tend to remember stories more than any other element.

Digital storytelling

Digital storytelling is a relatively new term to describe how the Internet is used to relate and spread stories. Here, the classical format of storytelling tends to be replaced by a combination of photos, videos, sound, and text, often used interactively.

Digital storytelling may be used, for example, in education, health information, and by museums. Many companies use it for marketing, attempting to reach potential customers through a variety of Web-, mobile-, social-, and email platforms. On the one hand, customers are invited to relate their experiences with the product, which can then be passed on to other users; on the other hand, companies also attempt to generate attention by introducing their own "stories" into the digital arena.

Storytelling in training

Storytelling is also experiencing a boom in the field of seminars and consulting. In 2012, Managerseminare magazine hailed storytelling as the "rising star" among training and consulting methods (www.managerseminare.de/blog/trainingsmethoden-2012-shooting-star-storytelling/2012/07, accessed 12 July 2018). Storytelling can be used in many ways in training sessions:

- Trainers can build stories into their presentations to deliver their messages in an absorbing and lively way.
- Storytelling can be proposed as a method in workshops on presentation techniques, and communication.
- When people have worked together to build up a story, this can be of enormous benefit to team development.

The following sections show how to make this possible.

Building stories

To be able to tell interesting stories, and to deploy them effectively, we need to know how stories are built up in the first place. This applies equally to stories from our experience, stories we have heard from others, or those we have made up ourselves. The technical term relating to this is "dramaturgy," from the Greek for "drama" and "worker," meaning dramatic composition. Dramaturgy teaches how narrative methods and elements are chosen and arranged to represent a story. Stories may be closed or open in form; closed stories encompass an entire plot from start to finish, whereas open narratives may cover several threads, and may not necessarily end by wrapping up the conflicts and problems presented. Aside from books, films, and stage productions, closed narrative formats are more suitable for storytelling, as they are simply structured, and offer a clearer overview.

There are three essential elements in closed narrative:

Act 1 (exposition) – introduction/initial situation: the characters and the starting point for the story are introduced.

Act 2 (confrontation) – main body and events: something happens, "the plot thickens," and tension is built. Towards the end of this part, the story reaches its dramatic climax.

Act 3 (dénouement) – closing/result: the tension and conflict are resolved.

The German author Gustav Freytag (1972) and the American non-fiction writer Syd Field (1991) offer two descriptions of how stories are built up:

Table 7.1 Dramatic structure. Two versions, from Freytag and Field (Mod. from Freytag, 1972; Field, 1991)

	Gustav Freytag's five-part pyramid model	*Syd Field's three-act structure*
Act 1	**Exposition:** All principal characters, protagonists and antagonists, the settings, and the trigger for the dramatic tension are presented. However, this trigger need not be explicit.	The characters are introduced in their settings. The **setup** is delivered, and the "inciting incident" occurs.
Act 2	**Rising action:** The situation becomes more critical, and further complications prevent any solution to the conflict.	The **confrontation**, whereby the protagonist(s) must face conflicts from within themselves and/or from outside. Unexpected events occur, conflict breaks out, and the protagonist(s) must react to it.
Act 3	**Climax:** The tension reaches its zenith, as the plot and the conflict are driven to their peak.	**Resolution** of the conflict.
Act 4	**Falling action:** The brakes are put on, and one side gains an upper hand. At this point a final moment of suspense may be introduced, temporarily increasing the tension again by putting the final outcome at risk.	
Act 5	**Resolution:** The conflict is resolved.	

However, a story does not consist only of a structure; it is brought alive by its dramatic arc. For a story to be interesting, it requires the following elements (Cossart, 2017):

A **protagonist** to deliver the story (the hero in the hero's journey, whom we will meet below).
This character needs **a direction, a goal**.
Difficulties or conflicts that initially prevent the protagonist from reaching their goal.

The protagonist's striving towards the goal determines the dramatic style. The goal spans the entire dramatic arc, from the beginning to the end of the story. If this goal could be reached without effort, before the action even got going, the story would be dull, so obstacles and conflicts must be placed in the way. The story becomes exciting when we want to know what will happen. These obstacles and conflicts may be internal to the main character (e.g. I want to change something, but I don't have what it takes). They may be in the form of personal conflicts with other characters (e.g. I want to change myself, but my family is standing in my way). Or these conflicts may be with institutions, laws, or the environment (e.g. I want to change something, but the law forbids it).

Additionally, more profound stories will differentiate between the protagonist's conscious goal (the "want") and an unconscious desire (the "need"). Ideally, this unconscious need will be universal, resonating with the audience by tying in their own desires and aspirations. A "classic" of this differentiation is a striving for success and the underlying longing for recognition. Such stories are enthralling because they mirror our own questions, concerns, targets, and so on, and we see how the fictional or real character deals with them. The character becomes a model for us, and serves as a "mental testbed" for us.

The hero's journey

The American linguist and literary theorist Joseph Campbell developed an influential perspective on stories and symbols in his work on mythology and religion. Campbell conjectured that at their core, all of this Earth's mythologies and religions spring from and reflect "universal experiences," which he termed the "monomyth." Heavily influenced by Carl Gustav Jung's depth psychology, Campbell sought to identify universal structures in humans' lives. He posited that the actions of the main characters of stories – the hero of myths, novels, and films – represent the "hero's journey." This is characterized by an archetypal basic structure, sequence of events and characters, and outlines an idealized process of a person's development and maturity.

The hero's journey distilled elements from both within and outside the spectrum of mythology, that is, essential human questions, which the protagonist must address. Another example of this "recipe" of development in the form of stories is the classic coming-of-age novel, which presents the psychological and spiritual development of the main character through the barriers that she must surmount. Her successes and failures and how she learns from them describe the process of her personal development. Some of many fine examples from literature are William Meister's *Apprenticeship* (Goethe, 2009, 1795), *Demian* (Hesse, 1974, 1919), *The Lord of the Rings* (Tolkien, 2007, 1945–1955), and, more recently, the Harry Potter series (Rowling, 1997–2007), or *Eragon* (Paolini, 2004–2011).

The United States film industry has been heavily influenced by the pattern of the hero's journey, particularly through the "story development" work of the Hollywood development executive Christopher Vogler at 20th Century Fox. Vogler believes that emotional and spiritual dimensions are essential for a story to be "good," and for it to continue influencing the audience. In his book "The Writer's Journey" (Vogler, 2007), he describes the universality of storytelling structures, largely based on Campbell and Jung. Even though Vogler simplifies the structures for his own purposes, he still puts his protagonists through a variety of challenges, problems, and tests on their journeys as individuals. This form of the hero's journey is everywhere in Hollywood, and countless films have been built on the pattern, from "East of Eden" to "Rocky," "Star Wars," "Pretty Woman," "Lion King," "Finding Nemo," and so on.

Vogler's version of the hero's journey differs little from the story structures described earlier. His hero's journey is also split into three parts:

1   **Departure**
2   **Initiation**
3   **Return**

Particular features here are that the procedure is described in some detail, and that the Vogler model (2007) follows the pattern below:

Ordinary world: The heroine lives in her everyday world, and is more or less satisfied with it. She is usually something of an outsider, and notices that there must be more to life "out there."

Call to adventure: This tension and an initial glimpse of an unfamiliar world start preparing her to head off into an adventure.

Refusal of the call: As the heroine has learned to avoid risk, she initially tries to ignore the call to action. However, she knows deep down that she must follow the call if she is to fulfil her dreams.

Meeting the mentor: The heroine comes across her true mentor, who knows both worlds, and who stands beside her with actions and advice.

Crossing the threshold: Getting over the initial hurdle requires courage and willpower. There is now no way back for the heroine. The new world is very different to the old.

Test, allies, enemies: The heroine must grasp the rules of the new world, and learn to tell friend from foe.

Approach the innermost cave: The heroine gradually comes to understand "the big picture." She faces not only her archenemies and antagonists, but also comes to recognize the demons within herself.

The ordeal (death and rebirth): The main turning point of the story, bringing the greatest, irreversible change. During the life-and-death battle, the heroine must also face up to her own "dark side," and conquer it.

The reward (seizing the force): After the "rebirth," the heroine can look back with satisfaction on what she has been through.

The road back: With her new experience and knowledge, the heroine returns to her old world.

The resurrection: All the heroine's positive characteristics tie together with what she has now learned. In the final battle, she must no longer fight for her own well-being, but for the whole world.

The return with the elixir: The "elixir" is the integration of the heroine's experiences into her daily life, to enrich it and simplify it. The heroine has succeeded in her mission.

Figure 7.2 © Evi Fill

The ups and downs of the hero's journey will always improve the hero as an individual. The hero will usually be a completely "normal" person, with strengths and weaknesses. What makes him into a hero is that he faces real difficulties in his life, he conquers them, and thus becomes a better person. It is this change that is so fascinating, and this theme is an inexhaustible and well-loved element in stories. The psychological reason for this is that we project our own developmental processes onto such stories of change; the stories then offer us potential solutions, and become a template for our own betterment in "real" life (Bischof, 2004). The more clearly our own wishes, desires, and needs for improvement are held up to the light in the story, the more closely we will identify with that story, and the more gripping it will be for us.

Therapists and coaches have grasped this power of stories, and have further developed the hero's journey into a **psychological and therapeutic method**. The American director, actor, and trainer Paul Rebillot developed Gestalt therapy group seminars based on a therapeutic ritual.

The hero's journey is a favourite theme in the world of commerce, reflected in the myths and legends surrounding certain companies and their founders (e.g. Steve Jobs and Apple). We very often hear stories about "garage start-ups," which sometimes literally start in a garage, before becoming extremely successful. Alongside Apple, many other companies such as Disney, Delta Airlines, and Google carefully curate the stories of their humble beginnings.

Building up stories in improvisational theatre

In improvisational theatre, stories are generated on the spur of the moment, right there on stage. Players and audience both play a part, as the story is often built up from audience members' suggestions. For this to work, it is essential that stories have a clear and simple structure; furthermore, these structures and their rules must be so firmly ingrained in the players that they can draw on them at any time.

One story-creation structure that is known to work particularly well is Kenn Adams's "Story Spine."

Table 7.2 "Story Spine" (Mod. from Adams, 2007, p. 27)

Beginning: The start establishes a routine.	"Once upon a time ..." "Every day ..."
First significant event: Something breaks the routine.	*"But one day ..."*
Middle: The middle of the story shows the consequences, and increases the tension.	*"And because of that ..."* *"And because of that ..."* *"And because of that ..."* (Repeat as necessary)
Climax: The resolution is at hand.	*"Until, finally ..."*
End: A new routine is established.	*"And ever since then ..."*

As before, this story form may be reduced to three core elements:

1   **There is a routine.**
2   **This routine is broken.**
3   **A new routine begins.**

Here is an example:

> *Once upon a time there was a manager, who loved his work above all else. Every week he worked a great deal of overtime. But one day, his wife told him she wanted a divorce. And because of that, he realized that he loved his wife even more than he loved his work. And because of that he quit his job and tried to get his wife to change her mind. And to do that, he sent her a hundred roses every day. And because of that he soon ran out of money. And because of that he started instead to draw a flower for his wife every day. Until, finally, his wife realized that she still loved him. And ever since then they have stayed together, and have started a flower shop, in which they also sell drawings of flowers.*

Adams (2007, p. 23) lays out the following structure for story creation:

- **Beginning** (25 per cent of the whole story)
- **First Significant Event**
- **Middle** (50 per cent of the total time)
- **Climax**
- **End** (25 per cent of the total time).

At the start of the story, all the main elements – which should all retain their significance at the end of the story – are introduced. The idea is to "keep these elements handy," to be able to bring them back later in the story. For example, if we see a scarf at the start of the story, and later on we have a murder, then perhaps that scarf was the murder weapon.

In the second part of the story, it is rare that any new characters or objects will be introduced. Through the "reintegration" of the elements introduced at the start, we feel that the story is nicely rounded, and we love it when objects which initially seemed insignificant turn out to indeed have a role. This carries over into our own personal stories, whereby there is a risk that our stories are replayed as close to reality as possible, so that side-stories and insignificant events will also be brought in. To avoid this, real stories must also be told in an enthralling way, and restricted to the most important elements. Kenn Adams's structure offers us an effective pattern for building up our stories in this way.

The following is a story from my own life as an actor, to which I often relate, and which I have structured according to the above model, but without constantly starting each sentence with the same words:

> *This story takes place in a theatre in Vienna. We were giving an impro-visational theatre performance. The show was sold out, and there was a great atmosphere. Everything was going wonderfully, and everyone was laughing. Then we came to the "No S Game," in which the players were not allowed to use the letter S. The audience suggested a location, and the players arranged themselves on stage. The first player then took a deep breath, and launched into the scene with, "So . . ." With that, the game was over before it even began, and the audience fell silent. The player became crimson with embarrassment, and we could all see how uncomfortable he was to have failed like that. But this then started the audience off laughing, until they were rolling in the aisles. The show was a great success.*

Stories should always convey a message. I like to tell this story in my seminars to help participants get over their fear of failure. The message here is that making mistakes is an essential part of improvisation, and that it is not only fun, but may even be the "icing on the cake."

Here are some exercises for practising storytelling:

Exercise

Three-line stories

Three players work together to come up with a story that is made up of only three sentences. The first player kicks off the story with the first sentence, the second player adds a second sentence to introduce the problem (the middle of the story), and the third player adds a final sentence to end the story.

Exercise

Raising the stakes

Three players are needed. Player 1 makes an offer, and Players 2 and 3 raise the stakes, e.g.:

Player 1: "*Andrea is driving in her car.*"
Player 2: "*She hardly slept last night and is very tired.*"
Player 3: "*Her baby is screaming in the back of the car.*"

The promise

The challenge with each story is to keep the attention of the audience from the beginning to the end. They will be gripped by the story if they want to know what happens next, and how the story will turn out. The principal theme of the story will usually be clear very early on, usually at the point of a "yes or no" question. We call this a "promise." The promise introduced at the start of the story must be honoured at the end.

For example, if a story starts like this:

> *Thomas walks through town every day to get to work. One day, walking along the pavement, he bumps into a young woman.*

The promise of this story, of course, is the question of whether Thomas and this woman will get together – yes or no?

Here is another example:

> *A marmot called Felix lives high up in the mountains. Every day he goes off to look for food, and squeaks to warn the other marmots of any danger. One day, a golden eagle suddenly appears overhead . . .*

This time, the promise is whether Felix can warn the other marmots in time – yes or no?

Here are some well-known promises from the cinema:

- E.T.: Will E.T. get back home to his planet? – Yes or no?
- Titanic: Will Jack and Rose survive when the ship sinks? – Yes or no?
- Harry Potter: Will Harry Potter vanquish Lord Voldemort? – Yes or no?

When the promise is honoured – that is, when the "yes or no" question is answered – the story is over. In other words, to the "yes or no" question at the start comes a "yes or no" answer at the end. To make it to this answer, the characters must face dangers and overcome obstacles between them and their goal – otherwise, the audience will lose interest in their story.

What to avoid in storytelling!

Up to now, we have seen how a story can be made exciting. There are, however, many ways in which a storyteller can quickly lose the audience.

With the help of Little Red Riding Hood, Keith Johnstone came up with several examples of how this may happen. (Johnstone, 1999, pp. 101–129)

Blocking

> *Will you take these cookies through the forest to Granny, please?*
> *But she's gone on vacation, Mummy.*
> You block when you want to stay in control.

Being negative

> *Will you take these cookies through the forest to Granny, please?*
> *But Granny nags all the time and she smells awful.*
> *Now, you know she can't help it.*
> *And it is raining.*
> Being miserable minimizes the transitions the hero will have to make when something bad happens, whereas starting positively would maximize them.

Wimping

Little Red Riding Hood meets the wolf but doesn't tell him about Granny.
We wimp when we accept ideas but refuse to add to them.

Cancelling

Little Red Riding Hood sees the wolf and runs home – nothing is achieved.
Cancelling dismantles whatever has been established: you light a fire and a
   shower of rain extinguishes it.

Joining

What big teeth you have, Grandma?
All the better to eat you with!
Well, my teeth are as big as yours, so watch out!
Having the same reaction as your partner is a way to avoid tilting the balance.

Gossiping

Do you remember when the wolf gobbled us up, Granny?
Oh yes, it's lucky that the woodsman was there.
Gossip avoids interaction by discussing things that are happening elsewhere,
   or at some other time.

Agreed activities

*Little Red and the wolf play hide-and-seek and spin-the-turtle, then they
   practise ballroom dancing.*
The characters seem to be working well together, but no one is in trouble, and
   no one is being altered (except for the turtle).

Bridging

*Little Red keeps postponing the meeting with the wolf so as to have something
   to fall back on.*
Bridging describes the building of bridges over streams that could be crossed
   in one stride. Asked to fire an employee, a boss might say, "How long have
   you been driving buses for us, Jarvis?"

Hedging

What will you say to Granny, dear?
I'll think about that as I walk through the forest, Mummy.
Hedging is like bridging, except that instead of postponing a good idea you
   waffle in the hope that you might think of one. But you won't, because this
   is not a creative strategy.

Sidetracking

Little Red Riding Hood glimpsed a wolf through the trees, but at that moment she fell down a deep hole.

Being original

Little Red Riding Hood is about to step out of the house, when she's hit by a ton of spaghetti.

This is a form of sidetracking in which the improviser expects to be admired for dragging in clever irrelevancies.

Looping

Little Red picked some primroses and some violets and some bluebells and then she picked some berries and some mushrooms and then . . .

If this continues she'll never meet the wolf. This may get laughs, but while they're spiralling like this, nothing is happening.

Gagging

Little Red Riding Hood peers into a glass that contains Granny's dentures, and says, "What big teeth you have, Grandma!"

A gag is a laugh that you get by attacking the story.

Comic exaggeration

Take these cookies to Granny, and these apples, and this haunch of beef. Oh, and you'd better take the refrigerator, and don't forget this set of encyclopedias . . .

This pointless exaggeration kills any interest in what will happen, so now the jokes will have to be really good. His conscious intention was to be amusing, but his unconscious intention was to avoid an emotional transition.

Conflict

Where are you off to, little girl?
Go away, I don't like to talk to wolves.
Come here!
Ow! You're hurting my arm. Take that! And that!
You little brat! I'll bite your head off! Ow! Ow! Stop kicking my shins!

While this is going on, the story is stalled (and it weakens the suspense if Little Red perceives the wolf as dangerous).

Lowering the stakes

Little Red Riding Hood makes no attempt to escape: "Get on with it then," she says, checking her lipstick in the mirror. "I've been eaten a lot of times, but the woodcutter always takes me home afterwards."

> One way to minimize trouble is to lower the stakes; for example, to change to
> "a silly magic trick," when it could have been "an amazing magic trick."

Keith Johnstone focuses here on changes happening in the story. The bigger the change, the more interesting the story becomes. But many people are afraid of change – even when it is only acting on stage, or telling stories – so they try to minimize change wherever they can.

Storytelling for companies

Companies are also increasingly using the power of stories, for example in their brand storytelling. This is the story of the origins, values, and visions of a brand, with the aim of strengthening customers' connection and loyalty to a product or a company. How a story can create an entire legend around a company and its founder – and how much money can be made from this – can be seen in the case of Apple and Steve Jobs. Every company has its own story; the important thing is that the story told should be essentially true and thus believable, rather than simply being made up for branding purposes.

Following are several kinds of stories that are useful for companies.

Founders and origins

These are stories about the pioneers that start a company. One example is that of the "garage start-ups" mentioned earlier, with Apple at the head of the list. The story of Steve Jobs is absolutely a "hero's journey," and this is what makes the story so popular. Jobs was adopted as a child, and was a student dropout, before he got together with Steve Wozniak to found the Apple company in a garage. He was later forced out of Apple, to start again from zero, before being brought back in 1996 to put the company back on its feet, then to the top of the game. Adopted child and student dropout to one of the most successful entrepreneurs of all time – and who was even thrown out of his own company, only to return and show everyone how it's done . . . Does it get any more "hero's journey" than that?

The company Steiff also has a rather lovely "origins" story. As a toddler, Margarete Steiff contracted polio, which left her partially paralysed, and she used a wheelchair for the rest of her life. In those days, a professional career seemed out of the question for her. However, in 1877 she opened a small shop, and sold clothing that she had sewn herself. She soon used a sewing pattern to make an elephant out of felt. This was intended as a pincushion, but actually made a fine toy, and led to the company's great success. Steiff began producing other animals, under the motto "Only the best is good enough for children." In 1897, her nephew Richard joined the company, and created a cuddly bear. This toy came to prominence when the United States President Theodore (Teddy) Roosevelt, on a hunting trip, refused to shoot a bear that had been caught and tethered for him. A caricature cartoon of the event appeared in *The Washington Post*, and the bear became a symbol for Roosevelt, known as the "teddy bear." The teddy business boomed, and the Steiff brand became famous around the world. Not only do stories like this remain in the memory for a long time, but they also communicate the values and beliefs of the company.

Success stories

Success stories function as models to follow, presenting success as stemming from a specific plan. One example is the electric sports car manufacturer Rimac.

Croatia is not exactly famous for its car industry . . . because until recently it scarcely had one. However, Mate Rimac has pulled off the impossible: his company Rimac builds electric hypercars in Croatia. As a child, Mate Rimac loved cars, and at 18 he bought his first BMW E30. At 20, he got it into his head to build the best sports car in the world. He started tinkering with his BMW, fitting it with an electric motor, and thus taking the first step towards founding his own company. He kept refining his BMW, until in 2012 he made the world record for the fastest quarter mile in an electric car.

Rimac went on to develop the Concept One, a hand-built electric hypercar with over 1200 hp, and which reaches 100 km/h in 2.5 seconds. The car is built from the ground up – including the batteries, drivetrain, and software – in the Rimac factory. This situation did not come about entirely by choice: suppliers are unwilling to deal with Rimac, or they set their prices too high, because the company is so small. It is also particularly difficult to find personnel in Croatia with the relevant experience in the industry. This led Rimac to mostly employ "lateral recruits" who are tinkerers like himself, such as Zvonimir Sučić, whom he brought in after seeing a downhill mountain bike Sučić had built himself. Many Croatians have relatively little money, and are used to being inventive and building things themselves, and this means that Rimac's team is made up of highly motivated and very creative individuals. Of great importance to him is the exchange of ideas between employees, which is encouraged at presentation evenings where anyone can talk about what he is working on at the moment. Meanwhile, Rimac has developed the Concept Two, whose 1900 hp takes it to 100 km/h in under 2 seconds. What will become of Rimac and his company is still unclear, but to build such a sports car company from nothing in Croatia – or indeed anywhere – is a great success story.

We can see that in both origin stories and success stories the foundations for the achievements were usually laid at the very beginning. However, it is the success stories that carry the greatest detail about the actual road to success.

Stories of change

These stories are all about difficulties, challenges, and crises that a company has overcome. They may also cover successful change processes, mergers, takeovers, or other major upheavals in the business.

IBM, for example, has been through a great deal. The company traces its origins back to a business founded in 1896 by Herman Hollerith, whose main activity was recording and processing data – such as voting cards in United States elections – using punch cards. After it merged with several other companies, the firm was renamed "International Business Machines Corporation" in 1914, focusing on hiring machines out to businesses. The 1950s saw the development of IBM's first computers and printers. When Apple brought out their Apple one computer in 1981, IBM countered with its first personal computer (PC) in the same year.

This move into personal computing represented a great breakthrough, in part because IBM chose to use processors from Intel and software from Microsoft. However, this clever manoeuvre was soon copied by other companies, leading to crisis at the start of the 1990s, as IBM lost several billion dollars (the largest company loss in United States history). A new CEO, Lou Gerstner, was brought in from outside the industry. He launched a radical cost-reduction programme, and began shifting the company's main business from hardware towards software and services. Within just a few years, IBM was firmly back in the black, a comeback that is still celebrated as one of the greatest in American business history.

The year 2002 saw IBM take over the auditing and consulting giant Pricewaterhouse Coopers, and in 2004 the PC business was sold to Lenovo in China, bringing an end to the original business model. Since then, IBM has focused on software and services, with great success up to now. In 2012, the company's leadership was taken over by a woman, Virginia Rometty, and in 2017 IBM chalked up a revenue of $22.5 billion in the fourth quarter. Today, the story of IBM is taught at universities of economics to illustrate how large companies can make it through great change.

Whether stories of a company's origins, successes, or changes, all these business stories still resemble the hero's journey, as they show how the organization proved its ability to thrive and survive in its environment. What obstacles were overcome, and what achievements were reached? The spirit of such stories can be used by any firm, giving it meaning, boosting motivation and team spirit, and providing a useful tool for marketing towards potential customers.

Storytelling in team development

Stories can be told not only by individuals, but can also be created through teamwork. However, this does require genuinely effective and close cooperation. In turn, the quality of the stories reliably reflects the quality of the collaboration. As explained in the "teamwork" chapter, certain storytelling exercises from improvisational theatre offer an excellent indication of the quality of collaboration in teams. For example, the "One-line Story" allows us to spot when and how stories are blocked, when somebody is negative, when they are sabotaging the story, and so on. Furthermore, almost all of Keith Johnstone's rules described above can be applied directly and practically in team meetings.

Here are a few examples of this:

Blocking

A "Yes, and . . ." generates a positive and motivating atmosphere, in which most people will want to play a part. If suggestions tend to be blocked, there is a risk that some will soon withdraw into themselves, and their knowledge and experience will be lost to the team.

Being negative

"That's never going to work," "We've tried that already," and other such examples of negativity also generate an atmosphere in which creative work and commitment are scarcely possible.

Wimping

When insecurity, fear, or tactical manoeuvring exist within a team, collaboration and team achievement are excluded.

Gossiping

Gossip is daily business in teams, particularly when conflicts or awkwardness are bubbling under the surface. Such talk will often be held back until the coffee break, where it can be used to fuel controversy. Since the content of these "private" (i.e. "stolen" from the public arena) conversations is restricted to a select few, it will rarely lead to an improvement in a situation, as its potential cannot be used if it is never brought to the table.

Agreed activities/everyday routine

Unspoken and often unchangeable routines can lead to lethargy and stagnance in teams, which simply rules out any innovation.

Imitation

In a team this can mean that nobody is giving their true opinion, and that they appear to be supporting others. For example, we may be afraid of triggering change or conflict, and having to bear the consequences.

Sidetracking

This also happens in teams, of course. We busy ourselves with irrelevancies and avoid acknowledging or tackling the genuine problems.

Being original and gagging

Being original at all costs may sometimes be confused with creativity. However, it is often damaging to collaboration, serving only to raise the profile of individuals. Bragging, forced laughter, hidden aggression, clowning around in the break, pretending to be jolly, and so on are all typical examples.

Instant conflicts/short-term problems

The intellectual pioneer of learning organizations Peter M. Senge (1997) wrote that organizations always concentrate on short-term results. This approach distracts us from the long-term, insidious change behind the results, and thus prevents us identifying the true causes of the problems.

Lowering the stakes

This tactic can be seen in phrases such as *"Yes, ok, fine,"* or *"I don't have a problem with that,"* which we use to acknowledge that a person is angry or disappointed. This often appears to be a good tactic when we are afraid of varied emotions. However, if we wish to nurture openness and trust in relationships in general – and certainly in teams – it is counterproductive.

Exercises for team development

If a team is to be able to tell a good story, every team member needs to be on board. It is particularly important that each individual be able to both take the lead and allow themselves to be led, and that they bring in their own stories, while also building on other team members' input.

Here are two storytelling exercises that are particularly useful in teams:

Exercise

Press conference

Four or five players sit on chairs on stage. The audience plays the part of journalists at a press conference. The players on stage are a successful group; however, they do not know what they are successful at. The journalists ask them questions that are as open as possible, for example, *"What was your last big success?"*, *"What are your upcoming projects?"*, or *"What's the secret of your success?"*

The players on stage answer these questions, and thus build up, piece by piece, what kind of group they are. Everything is possible: the first expedition to Mars, a rock band, the inventors of how to generate energy from rocks, and so on. The important thing is that no one player should build the story; it should come together bit by bit as the players build on each other's input.

This exercise shows clearly if collaboration is working. There are usually several who will hold back, not take the lead at all, and only offer trivial answers, while a few others surge ahead, intolerant of any uncertainty, wishing to fix everything in place right from the start. The aim, however, is to build up a group identity piece by piece, for example as follows:

Journalist: (a member of the audience): *"What's your most recent major success?"*

Player A: *"That was two years ago, when we were in China."*

Journalist: *"What are you particularly proud of?"*

Player B: *"We're particularly proud that, although we have such different specialisms as individuals, we still manage to work together so well."*

Journalist: *"What are your plans for the future?"*

Player C: *"We want to reinvent the Internet."*

Journalist: *"Tell us more about your latest project."*

Player D: *"It all began in Silicon Valley, when we all met at Stanford."*

Player B: *"That's right, and that's where we founded this great start-up."*

Journalist: *"How did you come up with the idea?"*

Player A: *"We noticed that a lot of mothers are actually very lonely."*

Player C: *"So we thought it might be a good idea to bring these mothers together and put them in touch with each other."*

Journalist: *"What did you call it?"*

Player D: *"Motherbook – Facebook just for moms."*

Journalist: *"And what's your recipe for success?"*

Player A: *"Motherbook is really successful in China, because the distances there are so great, and because a lot of mothers are home alone."*

Journalist: *"And what sort of things can you do on Motherbook?"*

Player C: *"You can swap tips about how to bring up your kids, get help with childcare, and get to know other moms."*

Player D: *"And the moms help each other find jobs."*

Journalist: *"Many thanks for the interview!"*

Another good exercise for this is as follows:

Exercise

String of pearls

Several players stand in a row on stage. Members of the audience give an opening line to the first player, and a concluding line to the last player. The players in the middle have to, one after the other, put a story together that leads from the first phrase to the last. They do this in sequence, and each player may only say one line.

Here again, the team must work together if they are to create a story that leads from the first line to the last. An example follows:

The opening line, given by the audience, is: "*It's a beautiful, sunny Sunday.*" The closing line is: "*It's great that it rained!*"
The opening: "*It's a beautiful, sunny Sunday.*"
Player A: "*Maria and Thomas are getting married today.*"
Player B: "*They've got everything planned out, and are very excited.*"
Player C: "*The weather is lovely, and the wedding reception is being held outdoors.*"
Player D: "*All the guests are sitting chatting at their tables.*"
Player E: "*Suddenly, it starts pouring with rain.*"
Player F: "*All the guests jump up and run indoors laughing.*"
Player G: "*The atmosphere is now even better than it was before, and everyone will have fond memories.*"
And now comes the closing line: "*It's great that it rained!*"

Figure 7.3 © Evi Fill

Storytelling in presentations

When we think back to our school days, what do we remember? Especially if this was a long time ago, there's a good chance we will only remember specific stories and unusual events – a legendary end-of-term party, a funny accident, a zoo trip that went awry, and so on. Ordinary, run-of-the-mill activities such as math tests are already lost in the mists of time. Even people whose heads are full of figures, dates, and facts will still remember proper stories more clearly. This makes stories an effective and captivating way of passing on information and making it come alive. The audience will be stirred up, and will make connections between the information and their own experience.

This very effectiveness means that stories must be handled with care, and the following questions should be addressed in advance:

Subject: What is the story about?
Excerpt: What is important?
Background: Why are we telling this story?
Context: Where and to whom shall we tell the story?

The presenter must have a clear idea of why she is telling the story, and what value it brings to the audience. It is important to think in advance about the core messages of the story, and how they relate to the subject at hand. What is the moral of the story?

We have at least three ways of building stories into presentations:

* Stories about ourselves
* Stories about the subject matter or the product
* Stories about others

Stories about ourselves

Stories that the presenter tells about herself may be compiled in the form of the hero's journey. Many people find it very difficult to come up with and relate true stories of a personal nature. We believe that our own lives are not exciting or interesting enough, and we are afraid of being perceived as narcissistic. And, of course, we are not always keen to reveal too much about ourselves. When we are looking for our own stories, rather than trying to think of straight successes in our lives, we should try to remember the times we successfully dealt with mistakes and failures. Just as with made-up stories, we need a principal character that people can relate to – ideally one who is less than perfect, and who has weaknesses, just like our audience.

A hero's journey story should convey how the hero gets the better of a situation that challenges her as a person. It should be frank, honest, and believable, and should bring the events and the crisis to life. Naturally, the story must link to the subject of the presentation.

Above all in the United States, personal stories such as these can often be heard, even at specialist congresses. People talk about how they got through divorce, how they beat alcoholism (e.g. George W. Bush), failed business ideas and other disasters. These stories feed the idea that the person – having surmounted these problems – is in a good position to speak about the subject at hand. In Europe, by contrast, people are rather more reserved about revealing such personal details in public; but this does not prevent personal stories from being an excellent medium through which to stimulate the emotions and interest of an audience, and to "draw them in." It goes without saying that the level of intimacy must depend on the person's own preference, the theme being dealt with, the cultural setting, and the audience themselves. We can remain on safer ground if we talk about our own professional calling, how we came to be in our career, in our job. Here is an example:

Example story

My name is Sandra Wagner. I spent my childhood, 50 years ago now, in Ofenbach in Styria, Austria. Ofenbach has only 500 inhabitants, and back then almost nobody went on to higher education. Women were expected to do some sort of job, before marrying and having children. I was very good in languages, and a good student all round; I really should have gone to grammar school, but never believed in myself enough. So after an apprenticeship in gastronomy, I worked in my future husband's hotel. I married young, and had two children, but was still able to carry on with my job – something my family didn't understand at all. As the children got older, a regular customer told me that he saw potential in me, and that I should go to college after all. That was an important moment for me, and I felt a strong urge to do something. However, my husband and everyone else around me were against it and couldn't understand it. There was also the question of money, and whether I could afford to do it at all. I had to get over a lot of obstacles, both from outside and within myself. But at a certain point it became clear to me that I was on the right road. After our divorce, I moved to Vienna and began studying tourism management, and also found that I had a passion for research. After I graduated I worked for many years in the field, before applying to become a lecturer at the college. After five years, I now head up the tourism management programme, which is a dream job for me. When I look back, I'm glad I had so much practical experience, which helps me bring theory and practice together, and which I think is very important in the work I do now.

The promise in this story is: Will she go further with her studies or not?

At the start of the story, the routine is described. The line "*As the children got older, a regular customer told me that he saw potential in me, and that I should go to college after all*" is the initiating event in the story. Then the risk is increased, with the line "*There was also the question of money, and whether I could afford to do it at all*" representing the zenith of the tension. The end of the story "honours the promise," and the tension is resolved. The moral of the story is also vital – why is this story being told, and what is the message? In fact, this story conveys several messages:

• We can overcome obstacles when we are ready to fully commit.
• Our journey through life has highs and lows, and unexpected changes of direction.
• Take yourself seriously and believe in yourself.
• Theory and practice are equally important.

Hero's journey stories can be told about an individual team, or the whole company – what did we have to overcome to reach our great achievements? This will increase people's connection to the company, their motivation, and their feeling of belonging. Such stories can even be used for marketing purposes.

Stories about the subject matter or the product

Concrete illustrations worked into stories link theory and practice, and so are plausible, believable, and easy to understand. However, this becomes more difficult if our content is very abstract, which in turn makes it even more important to identify suitable examples based on truth.

Example story

Frau Lang is a specialist in nursing care at a care home for the elderly in Switzerland. She also trains healthcare practitioners at a technical college, focusing on the causes and risk factors leading to pneumonia in older people. After covering the theory, she tells a "real-life" story from the home:

> *Frau Müller came to live in our care home five years ago. She was 78, and still quite independent. Then, two years ago, she had a stroke, and has used a wheelchair since then. Frau Müller's posture had always been rather hunched, but since she has been in a wheelchair this has become much worse, and her chest has sunken severely. This decreases the amount of air she gets into her lungs, and the circulation of blood to the lungs, and there is a significant danger that bacteria could build up there and trigger pneumonia. A year ago this did indeed happen, and Frau Müller's life was in danger. What made her situation even worse was that her granddaughter was pregnant, and Frau Müller*

> *desperately wanted to be alive to see her great-grandchild. She pulled through, and since then we have intensively been taking preventive measures against pneumonia, using breathing exercises and rubbing techniques to stimulate breathing. Frau Müller has always been very motivated and cooperative, and this has paid dividends. The question was, of course, if this would work in the long term, and how her health would develop.*
>
> *I'm pleased to say that since then she has never suffered from pneumonia again, and is generally stable. She gets regular visits from her granddaughter and great-grandchild. This was a great success story for all of us carers, and has resulted in our applying these methods to other patients with similar problems.*

The promise in this story is: Will Frau Müller get pneumonia or not?

Once again, the story starts by laying out the initial situation; then the first significant event comes with the line *"A year ago this did indeed happen, and Frau Müller's life was in danger."* The tension is then further increased to its high point with the phrase *"What made her situation even worse was that her granddaughter was pregnant, and Frau Müller desperately wanted to be alive to see her great-grandchild."* Then we have resolution at the end of the story, and an answer to our "promise."

The moral of the story is that it is well worth taking preventive measures against pneumonia!

Example stories can of course also be told about products. Most of the stories are about the difficulties that can be solved by using the product, and they can be told either by sales personnel or by customers themselves. The last few years have seen a real boom in customer stories being used to market many different types of products. A good example of this is the storytelling campaign of the pharmaceutical company Janssen in 2015. On the "Our Stories" section of their website they present the stories of patients (their "Storytellers") who have fought their way back to life, and who talk frankly about the health issues they have faced.

Stories about others

We can also tell stories about others, for example about other companies or departments. Once again, it is important to link the story to the subject at hand. Such stories, however, have rather less impact than stories about ourselves, as they lack the personal element, and thus a certain authenticity. But they may still be useful when we wish to illustrate a subject and bring it to life.

Example story

Herr Walter runs a large and up-to-now successful hotel in Switzerland. At a staff get-together he tells the following story:

As you all know, our booking numbers have been dropping over the last two years, and our financial situation isn't exactly rosy. We can all see that this is a difficult and worrying situation. One major reason for the drop in business is certainly the strength of the Swiss franc, but of course we can't do anything about that. So I've been looking at what we can change, and a couple of months ago I came across a hotel in Graubünden that has managed to get over this problem, and has been getting more customers year on year. The size and structure of that hotel is very similar to our own, so I went over there to find out what they were doing right, and to talk with their business manager. My main takeaway point was: find your focus, and invest in it! The hotel has specialized in family holidays, and has thrown everything they have into that. Another important point – and this of course should be obvious, but unfortunately sometimes isn't – is friendliness and service! Over in Graubünden they've done a lot of work on the way they talk and deal with each other – and not only with the guests, but also among themselves as staff members. If the staff are happy, this passes on to the guests. And when it comes to service, they work on the principle that "Everyone is responsible!" This means that if somebody asks a question or wants something, the staff member attends to that personally, either by doing it themselves, or at least by passing it on to the right person – within a fixed limit of two minutes! That sounds impossible, but it can be done if everyone does their best, and treats their customers as "part of the family."

I would like us to try a similar approach together, too. This starts with investment, and the bank has already agreed on a loan. As we've always had families here, I'd like to focus more on that. We've already made detailed plans, and you can look at those at the end. As for being friendlier, I'm going to lead the way myself so that we can be more agreeable with one another, and of course with the customers too. I've noticed that if someone makes a complaint, it often turns into a bit of a fight, so I want to avoid that in the future. In fact, there will even be special training on that. And as from now, we're going to ask customers personally for their ideas on what we can improve, and we'll act on those wherever possible. I believe in the future of our hotel, and I look forward to taking this road – which may be rocky at times – together with all of you!

The promise here is: Will the hotel survive?

The initial situation of the story is that the hotel is struggling. The event that initiates change begins with *"So I've been looking at what we can change, and a couple of months ago I came across a hotel in Graubünden that has managed to get over this problem, and has been getting more customers year on year."* The tension is increased by the question of whether this hotel can also follow this successful model. The story is open-ended, and the initial promise question will only be answered in the future.

The moral of the story is that a situation can be turned around when everyone pulls together.

Storytelling exercises for seminars on presentation techniques

Improvisational theatre offers us many exercises for practising storytelling as a technique in presentations. Here are some examples:

Exercise

Incorporation

All players move around the room. When two players meet, one of them gives three words as prompts, and the other player must come up with a story containing all three words.

This exercise is most effective when the players give each other feedback on how the story was constructed.

Exercise

Backwards stories

One player leaves the room. The other players place four objects on a line, around one metre apart. The player returns to the room, her eyes closed. The others help her to stand next to the end of the line, with her back to the objects. She now opens her eyes and begins telling the story. She walks backwards slowly, parallel to the line, and as soon as she sees an object she must immediately incorporate it into the story.

This exercise helps us practise telling stories spontaneously, and can also help us learn to deal with unexpected interjections or questions during a presentation. It is important not to stray from the theme of the story, while still retaining the flexibility to integrate new "objects" (interjections and questions) as quickly as possible.

PowerPoint Karaoke

PowerPoint Karaoke is an enjoyable spin-off from classic karaoke. It was developed in 2006 by the "Zentrale Intelligenz Agentur," a network of writers, journalists, and web designers in Berlin, and since then has become very popular. It is usually run as a public performance whereby volunteers from the audience must deliver a presentation using PowerPoint slides they have never seen before, and whose subject they are most unlikely to know much about. The presenter must try to tell stories that somehow fit the theme – these may be stories they have personally experienced, or that they have read or heard, or that they make up on the spot. PowerPoint Karaoke thus improves spontaneity and the ability to tell stories, and is of course an excellent training method for presentations.

Conclusion

Storytelling is one of humanity's core abilities, which has accelerated our development and remains extremely important to us despite the invention of writing. Aside from entertainment and the passing on of knowledge, storytelling has now also become a method with many applications. Good stories will almost always be based around change, and this will ideally reflect the audience's own desires for improvement. A story is effective when it stimulates and activates its audience to link their own memories and experiences with it, and to become curious as to how the story develops.

Here is a summary of three essential ways to deploy storytelling:

- Stories may be compiled jointly, an example being digital storytelling in advertising, where companies take and develop clients' own stories and experiences.
- Story compilation may arise from teamwork. Such joint efforts are a wonderful indicator of the quality of the collaboration in the team.
- Stories may be used to bring lectures and presentations to life and make them much more interesting.

The stories we tell get better the more often we tell stories!

Practical examples

"Communication and Presentation Skills Training,"
University of Liechtenstein

Main points

Organization:
The University of Liechtenstein is a publicly owned facility concentrating on architecture, regional development, and business economics.

Assignment:
An elective course on presentation techniques and communication

Duration:
One semester

Target group:
All students at the University of Liechtenstein

Goals:
Participants were to . . .

- professionalize their demeanour and presentation before others, so as to be able to present their ideas using natural speech, voice, and body language
- learn how to exhibit presence and charisma before others
- learn about the foundations of classic presentation techniques
- find out how to use inspiring stories from their own lives, to bring vitality and their own personality into their presentations
- improve their ability to plan public talks, tailored to their target audience
- develop strategies to deal with difficult audience members
- improve their spontaneity, creativity, and ability to react to unexpected situations

---

Initial situation and highlights

Since 2014, the University of Liechtenstein has been offering innovative inter-disciplinary courses for students to augment their specialist knowledge with improved negotiation competencies and the ability to reflect on their work. In times of changing working conditions and rapid technological advances, skills such as "joined-up thinking" and picking up new subjects quickly are becoming essential. The participants on these courses are graduates or postgraduates, and come from a variety of study disciplines and cultural backgrounds. The students are expected to deliver a presentation on every unit, with feedback from the other students and from me as lecturer. Other principal themes on this course are "status" and "storytelling." Under "storytelling," the students learn how to make their presentations more interesting and true to life.

One exercise we use is PowerPoint Karaoke.

Exercise

PowerPoint Karaoke

Preparation: each participant pulls PowerPoint slides from the Internet on a subject of their choice. They should choose around 10 slides, and the less the participants know about the subject, the better. One person then begins their presentation. True PowerPoint Karaoke is about being as funny as possible, but our form of the exercise requires presenting the content as convincingly as possible. Given that the participants have no expert knowledge of the subject, they must deploy other attributes, such as presence, charisma, self-confidence, and storytelling. And even though the aim is not to be funny, it is all usually quite amusing.

This exercise is not just about having fun, as the students also learn not to hide behind the PowerPoint slides. They train their ability to be spontaneous, their presentation, and how to bring their personality to the fore.

Customer feedback from Monika Litscher (Coordinator for interdisciplinary elective courses at the University of Liechtenstein):

By working on their own personalities and their presentation skills, young graduates at the University of Liechtenstein develop competencies for their future careers. The "Communication and Presentation Skills Training" module is a valuable tool for knowledge workers that enables students to overcome communicatively challenging situations in a complex and global world of work.

Team development "Frequentis"

Main points

Company:
Frequentis is an Austrian high-tech company working internationally. It develops and sells communication and information systems solutions for the safety-critical areas of air traffic management, and public safety and transport.

Assignment:
Team development through applied improvisation and storytelling

Duration:
One day

Target group:
Human Resources staff

Goals:
The participants were to . . .

- come into contact with one another, and welcome new members to the team
- get to know each other better and strengthen their feeling of belonging to a team
- learn about the "Yes, and . . ." principle as a key to teamwork and innovation
- enhance their readiness to experiment and open up within the context of the team
- expand their range of coping strategies for unexpected situations and difficult meetings

---

Initial situation and highlights

The head of Human Resources was very keen to support his staff in becoming the "Best Performance Team," so he decided to try something new by working with applied improvisation and storytelling. Weaving a story together as a team presented an almost paradoxical – and thus exciting – challenge: working together towards the goal that they first needed to define and develop. This would require top-level teamwork.

A major theme in the workshop was storytelling, and one exercise we used was "Press Conference." For this exercise, the participants had to come up with a story on the spur of the moment. Afterwards, we talked about what worked well, and not so well.

Other exercises were an adapted version of "Helping Hands" and "The Interrogation":

Exercise

Helping hands

One player takes on the role of an inventor, and initially leaves the room. The audience then specifies a new invention that would be very important to their company. The inventor comes back in, and puts his hands behind his back. Another player stands behind him and stretches his own arms out, thus "playing" the inventor's arms. A third participant plays a presenter who asks the inventor questions about his invention.

The aim is for the inventor to work out what he has invented. The player behind him will particularly help him with his gestures, and if necessary the presenter can also help by the way she asks her questions.

Exercise

The interrogation

One player leaves the room, and the audience decides on a "wrongdoing" she has committed. The misdeed should relate in some way to the company or organization – something that is strictly forbidden in the organization, or something taboo. The "perpetrator" then returns to the room, and is questioned by the bosses (played by two other participants). They ask her about her crime, and through their questions help her work out what she is accused of.

Both exercises require everyone to work very closely together to come up with a joint story. Additionally, these exercises bring themes from the company to the surface in a playful manner.

Customer feedback from Friederikos Kariotis (Director Human Resources):

As part of a series of measures aimed at improving our team, I very much wanted to invite all the team members to come together in a workshop setting where we could try to push beyond our normal everyday boundaries together. The aim was to experience together the many different sides of each individual, strengthen our already good foundation of trust, offer everyone the chance to come out of themselves and flourish, and to have some fun together.

The workshop really got us moving!

Every single person managed to push the envelope and expand their horizons. We really broke new ground, and our trust in one another demonstrably grew, even during the workshop itself. We have been better welded together as a team ever since. We often think about events from the workshop, and have a laugh together. What's more, the day inspired us not only to work better together, but also with colleagues from elsewhere in the organization.

When your team is already on a firm foundation, applied improvisation is a wonderful and effective method to take the next step towards becoming a "High Performance Team."

Exercises for storytelling

1 **ABC Game**

   Procedure: Two players improvise a scene, taking turns to develop a reasonably meaningful story together. The first line begins with A, the second with B, then C, and so on. If a player makes a mistake, she is replaced.

   Themes:

   Spontaneity: Not only must players immediately come up with a word starting with the right letter, but they must be able to build that into a sentence that fits the story.

   Storytelling: Despite having to concentrate on the ABC, the players still should not stray too far from the story.

2 **Backwards Stories**

   Procedure: One player leaves the room. The other players place four objects on a line, around one metre apart. The player returns to the room, her eyes closed. The others help her to stand next to the end of the line, with her back to the objects. She now opens her eyes and begins telling the story. She walks backwards slowly, parallel to the line, and as soon as she sees an object she must immediately incorporate it into the story.

   Themes:

   Spontaneity: The player must integrate the objects into her story as quickly as she can. She also practises reacting quickly to interjections, questions, or criticism in presentations.

   Compiling stories: The player practises compiling and telling stories.

3 **Breaking with Routines**

   Procedure: Two players work together. One lays out an everyday routine, and the other attempts to break it by introducing a problem; for example:

> Player 1: *"Andrea is writing an email."*
> Player 2: *"All of a sudden, a carrier pigeon flies in through the window."*

or:

> Player 1: *"Sebastian is doing his homework."*
> Player 2: *"All of sudden all his books fly up into the air."*

Themes:
> **Compiling stories:** This exercise helps us introduce problems to disrupt the routine established at the start of the story.

4   Conversation Wave

Procedure: Four or five players begin telling a story together; then one focuses on one detail or word from the story and starts telling their own tale built around it.

Themes:
> **Storytelling:** The players get used to telling stories whereby they assume full responsibility for the whole story. However, the previous story elements are there for inspiration.

5   Elevator Pitch

Procedure: Two people are together in a lift. During the short trip, one tries to introduce to the other their company, product, or business idea as convincingly as possible.

Themes:
> **Presentation:** Participants must be able to appear convincing in a very short time.
>
> **Status flexibility:** It is important to be able to balance our own status with that of the other person.

6   Helping Hands (in adapted form)

Procedure: One player takes on the role of an inventor, and initially leaves the room. The other players then agree on a new invention that would be very important to their company. The inventor comes back in, and puts his hands behind his back. Another player stands behind him and stretches his own arms out, thus "playing" the inventor's arms. A third participant plays a presenter who asks the inventor questions about his invention.

The aim is for the inventor to work out what he has invented. The player behind him will particularly help him with his gestures, and if necessary the presenter can also help by the way she asks her questions. The inventor will only work out the solution if all three work closely together.

Themes:

> **Accepting offers:** The players need to listen to each other and accept each other's offers.
>
> **Leading and allowing ourselves to be led:** The game is guided in turns by the inventor, the second player's arms, and the presenter. Each plays a part in slotting together the parts of the puzzle, and success is only possible if all three cooperate.
>
> **Teamwork:** Without teamwork, the inventor will never be able to work out what he has invented.

7   I am Tree: Compiling Stories

Procedure: All players stand in a circle. One goes to the centre and says, for example, "*I am a schoolgirl*," and thus kicks off the story. A second player comes and introduces the problem, by saying something like, "*I am a poor grade*." A third player might say, "*I am the epiphany*," thus offering the solution. There are never more than three players in the centre. Then the first player takes one of the others and says, for example, "*I'm taking the poor grade with me*," and both players go back out to stand in the circle again. The player left in the middle repeats what she is (in this case "*I am the epiphany*"). Now two more players come and build a new scene and story around those words.

Themes:

> **Accepting offers:** The previous player's offer must be accepted and built upon.
>
> **Compiling stories:** With just three lines the players practise compiling a story: introduction, problem, and resolution.

8   I am a Tree: Raising the Stakes

Procedure: One player goes to the centre and says, for example, "*I am a schoolgirl*." A second player now introduces a problem, adding, "*I am a poor grade*." Several more players then come and make the problem worse: "*I am fear*," "*I am the violent father*," "*I am the dead mother*," "*I am suicidal thoughts*," and so on.

Themes:

> **Compiling stories:** The players learn how to worsen the problem, raise the stakes, and thus make the story more gripping.

9   Incorporation

Procedure: All players move around the room. When two players meet, one of them gives three words as prompts, and the other player must come up with a story containing all three words.

Themes:

> **Compiling stories:** This is another exercise in building up stories.
>
> **Spontaneity:** There is no time to think ahead; the story must be generated on the spur of the moment.

10 **Inventing Characters**

Procedure: All players sit in a circle and develop a character together. They begin with a name, and each player then adds a characteristic:

Player A: "*Maria*"
Player B: "*Meier*"
Player C: "*funny*"
Player D: "*heavy smoker*"
Player E: "*is single*"
. . . and so on.

Themes:

    Accepting offers: A realistic figure can only be created when each person picks up the previous offer and builds on it.

    Teamwork: The players must work as a team.

11 **Paper**

Procedure: The audience members write phrases on pieces of paper and put these on the stage. Two players improvise a scene together by picking up the pieces of paper and building the phrases into the scene.

Themes:

    Spontaneity: Here again, players must build sentences as quickly as possible into the developing story.

12 **Press Conference**

Procedure: Four or five players sit on chairs on stage. The audience members play the part of journalists at a press conference. The players on stage are a successful group; however, they do not know what they are successful at, nor what their relationships are to one another. The journalists ask them questions that are as open as possible, for example, "*What was your last big success?*", "*What are your upcoming projects?*", or "*What's the secret of your success?*"

The players on stage answer these questions, and thus build up, piece by piece, what kind of group they are. Everything is possible: the first expedition to Mars, a rock band, the inventors of how to generate energy from nothing, and so on. The important thing is that no one player should build the story; it should come together bit by bit as the players build on each other's input.

Themes:

    Accepting offers: The players build on each other's offers, and thus create their own identities piece by piece.

Leading and allowing ourselves to be led: Players must push the story forward, and at the same time adapt to and build on the other players' offers.

Teamwork: Good teamwork is necessary to create the team's identity.

13 Raising the Stakes

Procedure: Three players enter the stage. Player 1 makes an offer, Players 2 and 3 raise the stakes; for example:

Player 1: *"Andrea is driving in her car."*
Player 2: *"She hardly slept last night and is very tired."*
Player 3: *"Her baby is screaming in the back of the car."*

Themes:

Compiling stories: This exercise helps us learn how to increase the risk and thus the tension in the story.

14 Speech Tag

Procedure: Four or five players come together, and one begins telling a story. The next continues compiling the story, and so on.

Themes:

Teamwork: All players must work closely together, and build off one another.

Storytelling: The players practise telling stories without having to take on responsibility for the entire story.

15 Storyvision

Procedure: Here, the Story Spine is used to relate a story about a person's own vision of the future. This vision represents the end of the story, and the Story Spine tells us how this future vision is reached.

Player:

There was once a woman, around 40, who was no longer satisfied with her job in a training company.

Every day she had to follow a whole list of company rules, with no freedom to carry out her work as she saw fit.

So one day she decided to branch out on her own.

And because of this, she earned a lot less money at first.

And because of this she worked night and day.

And because of this she was too worried to get to sleep at night.

And because of this she met up with everyone she knew.

And because of this she went to every conference and event connected to her work.

> *And because of this she started marketing herself professionally.*
> *Until one day a major client took the bait.*
> *And since then she has been very successful as a freelance trainer.*

Themes:

> **Compiling stories:** The players use the Story Spine to learn about story compilation, and can also find their own way to their own vision.

16 String of Pearls

Procedure: The players stand in a row. Members of the audience give an opening line to the first player, and a concluding line to the last player. The players in the middle, one after the other, put a story together that leads from the first phrase to the last. They do this in sequence, and each player may only say one line.

Themes:

> **Accepting offers:** The other people's offers must be accepted if the story is to reach its final sentence.
>
> **Leading and allowing ourselves to be led:** Depending on where he is in the line, a player must launch the story, link it or flesh it out, or round it off.
>
> **Teamwork:** The team must develop the story from the first line to the last to give it meaning.

17 The Interrogation (in adapted form)

Procedure: One player leaves the room, and the others decide what "wrong-doing" she has committed. The misdeed should relate in some way to the company or organization – something that is strictly forbidden there, or something taboo. The "perpetrator" then returns to the room, and is questioned by the bosses (played by two other participants). They ask her about her crime, and through their questions help her work out what she is accused of.

Themes:

> **Accepting offers:** The players need to listen to each other and accept each other's offers.
>
> **Leading and allowing ourselves to be led:** Once again, this game can only work if all participants work together to both take and relinquish the lead.
>
> **Teamwork:** Teamwork is vital if the perpetrator is to work out what her crime was.

18 The Story of Your Name

Procedure: Everyone tells the story about their given names.

Themes:

> **Contact and getting to know one another:** This game works well at the start of the seminar, as it lets everyone introduce themselves and

find out new things about each other, all while telling the first stories of the day.

19   Three-line Stories

Procedure: Three players work together to come up with a story that is made up of only three sentences. The first player kicks off the story with the first sentence, the second player adds a second sentence to introduce the problem (the middle of the story), and the third player adds a final sentence to end the story. For example:

Player A: *"Thomas is walking to school."*

Player B: *"He meets Sandra on the way, and suddenly doesn't want to go to school anymore."*

Player C: *"They decide to bunk off school."*

Themes:

Accepting offers: As in all good stories, offers are accepted and built upon.

Compiling stories: An excellent exercise for practising compiling stories.

Bibliography

Adams, K. (2007). *How to improvise a full-length play – The art of spontaneous theater.* New York: Allworth.

Bischof, N. (2004). *Das Kraftfeld der Mythen. Signale aus der Zeit, in der wir die Welt erschaffen haben.* Munich: Piper.

Cossart, E. V. (2017). *Story tells – Story sells.* 3nd edn. Bergisch-Gladbach: Lesedrehbuch .

Field, S. (1991). *Das Handbuch zum Drehbuch.* Frankfurt a. M.: Zweitausendeins.

Frenzel, K., Müller, M., and Sottong, H. (2004). *Storytelling. Das Harun-al-Raschid-Prinzip. Die Kraft des Erzählens fürs Unternehmen nutzen.* Munich: Hanser.

Freytag, G. (1972). *Die Technik des Dramas.* 2nd edn. Leipzig: Hirzel.

Goethe, J. W. (2009, 1795). *Wilhelm Meisters Lehrjahre.* Frankfurt a. M. and Leipzig: Insel.

Hesse, H. (1974, 1919). *Demian.* Frankfurt a. M.: Suhrkamp.

Johnstone, K. (1999). *Impro for Storytellers.* 2nd edn. London: Routledge.

Paolini, C. P. (2004–2011). *Eragon.* New York: Random House.

Schank, R. C. (2000). *Tell me a story: Narrative and intelligence.* 3rd edn. Evanston: Northwestern University.

Senge, P. (1997). *Die fünfte Disziplin.* Stuttgart: Klett-Cotta.

Spitzer, M. (2002). *Lernen – Gehirnforschung und die Schule des Lebens.* Berlin: Spektrum.

Tolkien, J. R. R (2007, 1945–1955). *The lord of the rings.* London: Harper Collings Publisher

Vogler, C. (2007). *The writer's journey: Mythic structure for writers.* 3rd edn. Chelsea: Sheridan.

Online source

Bussmann, N. (2012). Trainingsmethoden 2012: Shooting Star Storytelling. *ManagerSe-minare.de*. Available at: https://managerseminare.de/blog/trainingsmethoden-2012-shooting-star-storytelling/2012/07 [Accessed 12 July 2018].

Chapter 8

Presentation skills

Introduction to presentation skills

The earth would still be a flat disc, and the sun would still orbit around it. America would remain unknown to Europeans, and the moon would still be the ship that carries people's souls to the sun, just as was still believed in the late Middle Ages. It was people with extraordinary presence and the ability to sell an idea who shaped history, brought innovation to the world, and were the drivers of change. People who financed a fleet of ships for the Spanish royals, or convinced a nation in distress to undertake things not because they were easy, but because they were challenging, and because even the sky is not the limit.

The ability to speak before others and present ideas is fundamental if we are to convince others of our own convictions.

Figure 8.1 © Evi Fill

Front of stage in any performance and any presentation stands personality, as only this can create an atmosphere conducive to trust and real interest. Actors and improvisational theatre players have made appearing before others into their profession. Improv players even dare to go on stage with neither script nor plan, they do not know what their first line will be, and they must be able to tolerate this void. In such a situation, it really is best not to think ahead, but to stay entirely in the moment, in a state of complete openness to ourselves, our partners on stage, and our audience. This is a state that comes highly recommended for presentations too, and is the foundation for personal presence (being in this place at this time). A presentation is, of course, prepared – in the same way that an improvisational theatre actor is trained and prepared for their work.

In this state of enhanced attention, the personality becomes visible, trust becomes possible, and humour is generated – we are perceived as authentic!

Any professional appearance requires the integration of everything described in the preceding chapters:

1   Teamwork: A successful performance demands collaboration with the audience through empathy, interaction, and eye contact.
2   Creativity: Saying "Yes, and . . ." to our own ideas and those of the audience facilitates humour and resilience.
3   Storytelling: Stories let our audience create their own mental images so that our message will sink in.
4   Status: Status flexibility is key to a successful performance.

Improvisational theatre and classical acting bring us many methods and exercises to improve how we appear to others, which can enrich every performance and presentation. As there is already a great deal of literature concerning presentation techniques, the following chapter will concentrate on the most effective techniques offered to us by theatre.

We will focus on the following questions:

•   How do I use my imagination to put myself in the position of the audience?
•   How do I begin a presentation with "presence"?
•   How do I build and release tension and interest in a presentation?
•   How do I intentionally deploy status in presentations?
•   How do I use my voice and speech to get my message across?
•   How should I best cope with criticism?

Preparation

Goal and target group

If a presentation is really going to get through to an audience, it must ideally convey a central message. A good benchmark is: What can be said convincingly in one sentence is highly effective. But this is easier said than done – how do we differentiate "convincing" from "less convincing," or trivial from relevant information? We might say that effective messages are "transmitted" on three frequencies simultaneously. First, content: what the audience should know by the end of the presentation. Second, information oriented towards the theme: after the presentation, the audience should know what to do. Third, emotion: experience shows that this is the most important aspect; the audience must feel emotionally in good hands, engaged, and understood.

The core competence of a presenter is to put himself in his audience's shoes, so that he can choose the right content and cover it appropriately. Before his legendary radio addresses, United States President Franklin D. Roosevelt always took plenty of time (Alter, 2006). He imagined how the listeners would be "gathered in the little parlor," how they would listen to the address and talk with their neighbours about what he had said to them. This core competence is based on empathy and imagination, which are also vital abilities for good actors.

Preparation in the room

As already described in the chapter on "Status," rooms and spaces have their own status, and any room that we are unfamiliar with will have a higher status than ourselves. This means it is very important to get to know the room, become comfortable with it, and to assume an appropriate status in relation to it before starting the presentation. The banquet hall of a Baroque castle, the Audimax in a university, or a seminar room in an airport hotel all have a very different status and feeling, and a very specific atmosphere. Whether we are conscious of it or not, the room has an effect on its occupants, and a presenter can use this to establish a certain communal space within the context of the presentation.

The start

Naturally, we hope for an attentive and interested audience. After all, we have something to say, and we hope that what we have to say arouses interest. We cannot simply assume that our audience is already "warmed up"; in contrast, we would do better to assume that the thoughts in the people's heads are revolving around anything other than "*Wow, I just can't wait for the presentation we are about to see!*"

In fact, our audience is far likely to be thinking about things like this:

- What a day – I'm exhausted already!
- I mustn't forget to check my messages.
- Is my kid OK on his school trip?
- What's this presentation about again?
- I hope this isn't just a waste of time!

Questions like this will preoccupy your audience at the beginning. Now imagine starting your presentation as follows:

> "*Hello, my name is Dr Heinrich Meier, I'm an expert in photovoltaic equipment and I'd like to show you some of the benefits of this technology. Let's*

start with the look at how photovoltaic equipment actually works." The first
PowerPoint slide appears – seven bullet points . . .

Maybe it is Dr Meier's lucky day, and his audience – already desperate to buy
some photovoltaic panels – will hang on his every word right from the start.
But what if they do not? How can he get his audience on board and make them
curious?

A successful presentation consists of a presenter, a subject, and an audience. The presenter's job is to convincingly link these three elements. At the
start of a presentation it is thus absolutely vital that the presenter be able to
answer the following questions that may be in the back of the audience's
minds:

- Why's he talking about this subject?
- What qualifies him to do so?
- Is he credible?
- What does the subject have to do with me?
- What benefit am I getting out of this?

The last question is probably the most important, as people will only give up their
precious time and attention if they feel it is likely to be worth it to them. Aristoteles (1999) already established that the ability to convince people required an
interplay of ethos (credibility), pathos (emotion), and logos (logical argument) –
the three pillars of rhetoric.

- **Credibility (ethos)** depends on body language and a clear link between the
  presenter and the subject.
- **Emotion (pathos)** springs from the speaker's attachment to her public, which
  she will mostly achieve through human themes common to all.
- **Logical argument (logos)** is supported by facts and figures that connect the
  audience to the subject.

The following can help us start our presentations successfully.

Having someone else introduce us

In situations where it is important for us to appear with a certain level of prestige
and esteem, it is best to have somebody else introduce us:

> *Good evening, ladies and gentlemen. I'm very pleased to be able to introduce
> Ms. Susanne Schinko-Fischli. She is a lecturer at the University of Liechten-
> stein and the Zurich University of Applied Sciences, and is an expert on the
> subject of applied improvisation!*

However, as we will look at more closely in the section "Status and body language for presentations," a very high status is not appropriate for all target groups! This is because our connection to the audience is essential, and this can only be achieved when the content, motivation, and emotions of the audience feel right. This applies particularly to the start.

Stand and wait

Here is a technique that will almost always get the audience's attention: enter the room, take your position at centre stage, and say nothing. Even when people are still chatting and getting settled, say nothing. Look at your audience in a friendly way, and make eye contact with them. Once everyone is looking at you, you begin to speak.

The cool demeanour that is necessary if we are to stand there out in the open and wait requires courage and presence. We can use the following exercise to learn how to judge the length of time it is appropriate to wait at the start:

Exercise

Waiting at the start

A person stands before the group, as if at the start of a presentation, and says nothing. Those watching him raise their hand once they begin to feel bored. This is usually a lot later than the presenter himself would imagine.

Standing and waiting like this is usually enough to trigger the curiosity and attention of the audience.

However, such pauses also boost the presenter's status, and once again, this is not necessarily appropriate for all audiences. This is particularly the case if the audience members themselves have a somewhat lower status, and feel insecure. For example, at the start of a seminar on presentation skills, many participants may be nervous about presenting, so it is best to establish verbal contact with them sooner rather than later, to avoid increasing unnecessarily the participants' nervousness and insecurity.

Presence

Presence refers to a person's power to project themselves, and depends on being entirely in the moment (the here and now). As soon as our thoughts begin to stray, and we start observing ourselves (or, even worse, we criticize ourselves), our presence will start to fade. It is said that a good actor or dancer can hold her audience in thrall even when standing with her back to them. This is made possible by the presence exhibited by the entire body. Being present, then, means clearly perceiving ourselves, our surroundings, and our counterparts or audience.

Presence is not something we should strive to attain as a "permanent state," as this level of focus is tough to maintain. It is also unnecessary; what we need is to attract attention at the right moment – at that specific time when we are trying to maximize the impact of what we are communicating. We can train ourselves to recognize these moments, for example with the following exercise:

Exercise

Presence exercise

One player stands before the audience (without speaking or doing anything). As soon as a member of the audience becomes bored, that person should raise his hand. When more than half of the audience have raised their hands, the exercise is over. It is necessary to maintain the interest of the audience when we cannot say or do anything. It works best when we are comfortable on stage and when we do not let our own attention wander.

Many people become nervous when they have to appear before an audience or give special presentations. Nervousness may be seen as the adversary of presence. Nervousness stems from insecurity, fearful assumptions about what will happen, self-criticism, and a worry that we will let ourselves and others down. The further these worries bring us away from the here and now, and the more they carry us from the subject at hand towards our (irrational) fears, the more nervous we become. This will destroy our presence, as we are too wrapped up in our own thoughts. One solution is to drag our thoughts away from the (unknown, uncertain) future into the present. We can do this by concentrating on the room: the smell, the light, our contact with the floor, and so on.

On the other hand, a certain level of tension can help the presenter cope with the challenging tasks ahead – such as exposure, raised attention levels, or the unknown reaction of the audience – and to keep the external tension within himself. Furthermore, if we have reached the point where we are no longer nervous at all, then we are less likely to push ourselves, preferring rather to remain in our comfort zone. Actors and improvisation players believe that this is the time to change profession or think about how to regain their inspiration and creativity.

Interaction with the audience

The ability to interact with the audience is another core competence of improv actors. Improvisational theatre will constantly bring the audience into the action, particularly by getting their suggestions for the next scene. In Theatresports™, they vote for the scene they most enjoyed, and in some types of long-form theatre they may even be able to determine how the story turns out. This is one of the main reasons that improvisational theatre is so popular with audiences: one can be actively involved in the creative process. To this end, at the start of most improvisational theatre performances the audience is "warmed up" by a presenter, and the audience members become noticeably less inhibited about getting involved in the show.

Also before presentations the audience should be woken up and warmed up! There are several ways to do this:

Asking questions

What do you associate with the word "improvisation"?

Words will certainly pop into their heads, such as "chaos," "fun," or "challenge." This technique can be used at any time to bring the audience in. It also creates a connection between them and the subject, as they are made to think more deeply about it.

Finding things in common

Establishing what we have in common with others around a given subject is another way to get the audience involved. With a large audience, a good idea is to get everyone to stand up, then invite certain groups to sit down one after the other.

Here is an example from my symposium on the subject of creativity at the Kleine Kunstschule in St. Gallen: First, only those who came by car could sit down, then those who came by train, and finally all those in a relationship. This meant that the only people left standing were those who came on foot or by bicycle, and who were single – which was a nice chance for those people to get to know each other in the coffee break!

At a presentation on the subject of improvisational theatre, this could turn out as follows. First to sit down would be all professional improvisational theatre actors, then everyone who has at any time acted in improvisational theatre, then those who have seen an improv show. Left standing would be those who have never had anything to do with improvisational theatre; these people should be welcomed most warmly of all, for example by mentioning that it is always particularly interesting to see how people who have no experience of improvisational theatre will react to the presentation.

Exercises

As in almost any workshop, short exercises can be used to involve the audience. For example, these may be carried out with the person sitting in the next seat.

In a presentation on the theme of creativity, the following exercise can be useful:

Exercise

Ask a stupid question

Two players ask each other stupid questions, such as *"What does an elephant wear in bed?"* The other player must answer as quickly as possible.

In presentations on the subject of status, I often use the following exercise:

Exercise

High status/low status

Audience members can do this with their neighbour. They should introduce themselves, first using high status (e.g. a long, firm handshake, maintaining eye contact all the time), then low status (e.g. a limp handshake, scarcely making eye contact). At the end, they should talk about how they perceived the differences between the two greetings.

Mumbling group

A mumbling group involves small groups of people, and can be used to relax and activate participants. It works with any seating arrangement, and also with large numbers of people. Two to four participants "huddle up" to discuss a given question, for example: *"When do you improvise in everyday life, and how does that work out for you?"* or *"Do you already make your presentations interactive, and if yes, how?"* The groups are then invited to feed their main conclusions into the general debate.

Personal stories

As already discussed in the chapter on "Storytelling," personal "hero's journey" stories can enrich any presentation, and are a very good way to start off. The quicker the audience knows just who it is who is talking to them, what qualifies them to do so, and the quicker the presenter can establish credibility, the more likely it is that the audience will lend their attention, and that the presentation in general will be a success.

Let's return to Dr Meier and his photovoltaic equipment presentation. The title of doctor may afford him a certain credibility, but academic achievements alone are unlikely to be enough. The audience wants to hear a good story, ideally one with which they can identify. Dr Meier's story might go like this:

> *Hello! My name is Heinrich Meier. I grew up in quite modest conditions on a farm in southern Germany. We used to have a lot of power cuts at home, and I still remember how inconvenient this was for our parents, who had to look after four of us kids. When I was about 12, I started thinking about how we might use solar energy. My physics teacher took my questions seriously, and told me that there were such things as solar cells, and that great progress was being made in a field known as photovoltaics. With her support, I started carrying out all kinds of experiments at home, and ended up almost burning the barn down. I never lost my interest in the subject, and have now made it my profession, with the aim of helping towards a great breakthrough in providing reliable, inexpensive, and clean energy for all.*

This represents a short hero's journey story, to connect to the audience. True, personal stories usually get the audience "onside," and awaken their emotions. But what do we do if we were not fortunate enough to be able to choose our career path, and we are forced to make presentations on certain subjects against our will?

One useful technique is used by actors in certain situations. Now and then they have to "fall in love" with their fellow actors, who may not be exactly Brad Pitt or Jennifer Lawrence. When an actor has a partner whom they find unattractive, well, we can really call that work! He has to consider the whole person, and think about what he may like about them. Despite everything, he may find some small detail such as the hands, the person's way of moving, their agreeable nature, their generosity – it can be anything. He can then "fall in love" with these details, to help him act scenes of love convincingly with that person.

A similar technique may be applied to presentations whose subject matter we find less than gripping. Here too, the effort required is to try to get so heavily into the subject and look at it closely enough that we can find something in it that we can somehow like – or even love. This effort may not be worth expending for every little presentation, but for something more important it can certainly be worth it, because the audience can tell the difference.

Presentation structure

The overall structure of a presentation – an introduction, a middle, and a closing – remains sensible and standard practice. And of course it is very important that the presenter uses their talk to remain focused on a goal and to repeat their message. Furthermore, a presentation should be built up like a story, with high point of tension in the last third. The subject is introduced at the start, then the tension builds to a climax, until finally the different threads are drawn together at the end of the presentation.

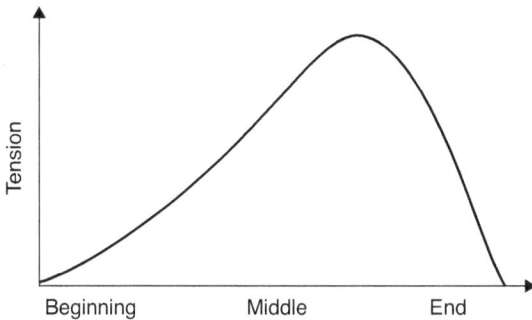

Figure 8.2 Tension arc in story structure, Susanne Schinko-Fischli

The presentation is most interesting when it maintains the audience's curiosity, because they never quite know what will come next. If we build in too much certainty, and start off by giving away the ending, then the audience's interest will nosedive. However, if we leave our audience to grope around in the pitch dark, they will also lack orientation during the presentation. So they need a little of both: a certain level of psychological certainty to allow them to relax a little, and just the right amount of uncertainty to keep them on their toes. This balance should really be achieved right at the start.

A classic example of this technique is Steve Jobs's presentation of the first iPhone (2007). He started with a digression, talking about other Apple products, before launching into the subject of the iPhone as follows:

> *[Pause] This is a day I've been looking forward to for two and a half years. [Pause]. Every once in a while a revolutionary product comes along that changes everything. [Pause]. And Apple has been, well first of all one's very fortunate if you get to work on just one of these in your career. Apple's been very fortunate. It's been able to introduce a few of these into the world. In 1984 [Pause] we introduced the Macintosh. It didn't just change Apple, it changed the whole computer industry. [Pause] In 2001 we introduced the first iPod [Pause] and it didn't just, it didn't just change the way we all listen to music, it changed the entire music industry. Well today we're introducing three revolutionary products of this class: [Pause]*
>
> * *The first one: [Pause] is a widescreen iPod with touch controls*
> * *The second: [Pause] is a revolutionary mobile phone*
> * *And the third: [Pause] is a breakthrough Internet communications device*
>
> *So three things, a widescreen iPod with touch controls, a revolutionary mobile phone, and a breakthrough Internet communications device. An iPod,*

a phone, and an Internet communicator. An iPod, a phone . . . are you getting it? [Pause]. These are not three separate devices, this is one device [Pause] and we are calling it iPhone. Today, today Apple is going to reinvent the phone [Pause] and here it is.

However, the slide does not show the new iPhone but an iPod with a turntable, which looks very old-fashioned and gets a big laugh from the audience.

Steve Jobs was a master at building excitement. The presentation begins with a personal connection ("*I've been . . .*"). He has been waiting for this day for two and a half years, so we know how important this day and this product are to him personally. And he starts "big," to raise excitement. It is not only a product; no, it is a *revolutionary* product, which not only changes many things, but changes *everything*. He then continues not by simply introducing the product, but by increasing the audience's curiosity by presenting three aspects of the iPhone without actually showing it, or even naming it. Through several repetitions, he hammers his message home. Jobs also intentionally builds pauses and humour into his presentation.

It is not for nothing that Steve Jobs was honoured by many, and considered a genius at presentations. In his 2009 book *The Presentation Secrets of Steve Jobs*, columnist Carmine Gallo describes how Jobs intentionally compiled his presentations as if they were movies, always with a story at the centre.

Not everyone is naturally predisposed to delivering fascinating presentations. But one very effective step towards it can be seeking feedback, to find out about ourselves and the effect we have on others, so that we can constantly improve, as follows:

Exercise

Tension Arc

Somebody is making a presentation or telling a story. Audience members raise their hand when the excitement starts to ebb. In this way, the presenter receives immediate feedback on the interest level in his presentation or story.

The leitmotif

The leitmotif is the subject of the presentation. Ideally, this theme and the message associated with it should be able to be summarized in one sentence. The leitmotif spans from one end of the presentation to the other, and holds everything together. It is not easy to "draw this bow," and in my seminars I can observe two types of presenter. The first believes everything to be important, can leave nothing out, and covers everything in minute detail.

For example, Student A: *"My name is Robert Hauser. I'm a student of architecture, and I come from Vienna, from the second district. In the second district we also have Prater, a huge park in the middle of the city. I grew up just near there. Vienna now has almost two million inhabitants, and is still growing . . ."* and so on.

Details can make a story interesting when they actually have something to do with the story. If they do not, such as in the story above, then they are irrelevant and will soon bore the audience. This student's details about his origins in Vienna would, however, be interesting if they were connected to an event in the story:

> *My name is Robert Hauser. I'm a student of architecture, and I come from Vienna, from the second district. In the second district we also have Prater, a huge park in the middle of the city. I grew up just near there, and spent much of my childhood around Prater. When I was still a kid I started thinking about how to make this park even more exciting for children. That's why I'm studying architecture, and it would be my dream project to remodel Prater.*

Cause and effect foundations for any story, and an exciting, unusual, and individual interplay between them will always grab an audience.

The other type of student does not flesh his story out at all, and simply runs through the facts:

> Student B: *"My name is Andreas Faber. I was born on 12.11.1995 in Erfurt, and I now study business administration. My specialty is customer behaviour, in particular certain types of reactions among customers."*

This presentation is unlikely to trigger any images in the minds of the audience. It is dull, and awakens no emotion at all.

Here is an exercise to help establish whether details are important and interesting, or simply boring:

Exercise

Colour and advance

This exercise requires two players. One begins to deliver a short presentation, or invents a story. At any moment the other player can say *"Colour,"* at which point the presenter must describe a person or object from the story in greater detail, until the observer says *"Advance,"* whereby the main presentation or story may continue. The observer should take his own genuine interests into account.

The following exercise can help us concentrate on the most important elements:

Exercise

Half-time presentation

The presenter must deliver her talk in half the original time, then in half the time again, and so on until only the very most important elements remain.

Status and body language for presentations

Basic position

The most important principle is: all eyes on the presenter. Her presentation depends on her presence and personality. It will fall flat if she – as the delivery medium of the presentation – lacks charisma and the ability to connect the subject matter with the audience, so that they are "drawn in."

The presenter must thus be clearly visible to everyone. She should balance her weight equally between both feet, with her hands around the level of her belly button. From this basic possession, controlled and calm steps and gestures may be made, which then attract attention and in turn boost authority.

In my seminars I often hear that consciously changing our body language no longer appears authentic. This ignores the fact that our own body language is largely something that we have learned. Indeed, it does feel very odd when we try out new postures, but this does not mean it is less authentic. Here again, it is important to gather feedback in order to compare the way we perceive ourselves to the way others perceive us. One possibility is to video a rehearsal – or even better, do it live!

Status

The basic position described above corresponds to a somewhat higher status. It communicates calm and control, and will make presentations more credible, and thus successful, because the presenter appears to be convinced of his own message. But once again, "bigger is better" does not necessarily apply, as a status that is too high can seem intimidating and unpleasant.

The "right" dose of status depends on the theme and the target group: Presenting the latest profit figures in a commercial company requires a wholly different status than announcing redundancies, or addressing the relatives of people with Alzheimer's disease.

As a first step, it helps to know about our own status. Every individual has a natural demeanour that tends to hover around a certain level of status, and can be identified through feedback, for example via the following exercise:

Exercise

Status feedback

A player comes on stage and tries to stand as "neutrally" as possible. Members of the audience call out a number from 1 to 10 according to what level of status they perceive in the player on stage. If desired, feedback may also be given as to how these evaluations were arrived at, that is, which signals and body language had the effect of raising or lowering the player's status.

And here is another great exercise to learn how to appear with a certain status:

Exercise

Status presentation

One player comes on stage, and a number from 1 to 10 is whispered in her ear (1 is the lowest status, 10 the highest). The player must then come to the centre of the stage and announce, "*Good evening, ladies and gentlemen,*" using the status level that was whispered to her. The audience must then guess which number she was given.

Surprisingly, almost anyone can manage this exercise, even "rookies" in the subject. Difficulties only arise when someone has to assume a status that is very different to their usual spectrum. For example, a person who almost always resides in a lower status zone may find it very difficult to act at status level 9. Respectful analysis and constructive feedback can then help clarify why it was so hard to reach level 9, and what the person may be able to practise to achieve that level.

If the group contains many participants who have trouble assuming a higher status, the following exercise can be useful:

Exercise

I am the director

One participant leaves the room, then comes back in through the door as the director/CEO of the company/university etc., and greets everyone in the room while playing this role.

This exercise tends to create much merriment, and it is always interesting to see people's different approaches to the role.

Eye contact

During a presentation the presenter receives constant feedback from his audience, either verbally (e.g. as interjections or as answers to questions) or non-verbally. Eye contact helps members of the audience feel like they are being addressed personally, and also allows the presenter to monitor whether they are still concentrating. Is the eye contact reciprocated? Are people starting to look at their phones? Are a few heads nodding already?

Through eye contact we can connect to the audience, draw them in, and react when we have still managed to lose them. We may, for example, say something like *"I'm noticing a little tiredness in the room"* or *"I can see a few confused faces . . . – or am I just imagining that?"* (Remember to maintain a friendly expression when asking such questions, so that they do not come across as a rebuke!) Then, when we get our answer, we can respect it and react appropriately.

The relevant literature concerning eye contact also contains tips on how to deal with nervousness. For example, we can look just slightly above the level of the audience, or we can imagine them all naked. However, these are avoidance strategies, and the audience will doubtless notice them, either consciously or subconsciously. So true contact with the audience remains the best means of countering nervousness, as it draws us away from our own fears and back to reality.

Voice

For an improvisational theatre player, the voice is an instrument every bit as important as the body, and it is a key element of any good presentation. Although the tone and volume of our voice depend on the characteristics of our vocal chords, the way we use our voice is learned, and can thus be changed. Since our voice is a determining factor in how we come across to our audience, the advice and support of a professional voice trainer or speech therapist can be invaluable. But there are also exercises to practise alone or with another person, and trainers can use these exercises in their seminars.

Posture and breathing

Once again, an upright posture and a balanced stance on both feet are important here. This position allows us to breathe freely, and is thus vital if we are to fully project our voice. If we wish to speak loudly and clearly without straining our vocal chords, we must be able to use the resonance of our own bodies to generate sound. The correct breathing technique creates space in the body for our voice to develop volume and power. Abdominal (diaphragmatic) breathing helps with this, and when we are relaxed, this abdominal breathing occurs automatically. Actors and singers learn how to intentionally "breathe from the gut" to give power to their voice.

The following exercises can make us more aware of our breathing:

Exercise

Breathing exercise with another person

Person A stands squarely on both feet. Person B moves around him and places her hands on various parts of his torso. Person A attempts to direct his breathing towards her hands. Then they discuss how it felt for Person A. Where could he "place" his breathing? Where did Person B feel it?

Exercise

Abdominal breathing alone

Place one hand on your stomach and the other on the upper part of your chest. At first, breathe normally, and feel how your hands move. If the upper hand moves more, this is chest breathing. Now concentrate on directing the breathing deep into the abdomen, towards the other hand. The belly should then move outwards, indicating abdominal breathing.

Voice quality

A resonant voice is easier to hear and listen to, is more convincing, and can fill a large room with sound. Controlled breathing as practised by singers is a useful technique to control the pressure of the breath, on which the tone and volume of the voice depend. The right pressure, controlled by the inhalation muscles, can generate a voice that carries well.

Playing a wind instrument can help us with this control. For example, we can try to hold a steady note on a flute. If the pressure is too high, we cannot maintain a steady sound, and if the pressure is too low there will be no sound at all. Controlled breathing is needed to regulate the flow of air.

To learn this control correctly requires time and, ideally, professional help. However, the following exercises can help non-professionals get a feeling for breathing control:

Exercise

Paper on the wall

Take a small sheet of paper and hold it against the wall at the level of your mouth. Stand around 20 cm back, and place your other hand on your stomach. Then let go of the paper and try to hold it against the wall by blowing it steadily. Your stomach should feel resistant to your hand. The longer you can hold the paper against the wall, the better you are already controlling your breathing.

Exercise

Breathing control

Stand upright, hands on hips. Pronounce a series of consonants loudly: "t, k, f, s, . . ." You should be able to feel the movement of the diaphragm as far down as the hips. After each consonant, the stomach moves inwards, then outwards to draw air into the lungs. The body inhales the air that it needs. This exercise can also be done with short words, such as "hey" or "stop," as if you were calling out to someone.

As with many speech exercises, the above one is not just about the physical technique, but also the intention. (In this case, we are imagining calling to a person who is far off.) This intention helps us bring the necessary power to the situation.

When we master controlled breathing, all the energy in the flow of breath is transformed into sound. We can test this by holding a candle before our mouth while we sing; the flame should not flicker.

If our breath cannot flow freely and our voice goes unsupported, it will usually sound strained and choked. In the long term this can lead to hoarseness and other signs of fatigue or damage to our voice.

Volume

On the one hand, the volume of our voice depends on speech and breathing techniques; on the other hand, intention plays a role – how much do we really wish to reach someone with our voice? If I call my son to come downstairs to the dinner table and he does not appear, it is unlikely to have anything to do with the volume of my voice; rather it will depend on his motivation. In private life we rarely speak too quietly, as we wish to be heard. But this is not necessarily the case in public speaking. Just as a nervous presenter may wish to make himself invisible on stage, in the same way he may not really want everyone to hear him (or indeed, not at all).

Actors, though, must constantly play to the cheap seats right at the back of the upper gallery. Presenters, then, should focus on the person furthest away, and monitor whether they are still following the presentation.

Articulation

Clear articulation (pronunciation) makes it more likely that we will be understood by every listener. The speech training offered to actors provides us with many exercises to improve our articulation. A classic example is the Cork Exercise.

Exercise

Cork exercise

Each participant is given a cork (or, even better, they use their thumb). Then, in pairs, they read a short text out loud with the cork or their thumb in their mouth, and then without. Each then comments on whether the other's pronunciation improved after using the cork.

This exercise can also be practised just before a presentation. Pronunciation will soon improve noticeably.

Naturally, we can also use tongue twisters to practise speaking clearly, such as the following:

Betty Botter bought some butter, but she said the butter's bitter.
If I put it in my batter, it will make my batter bitter, but a bit of better butter will make my batter better.
So 'twas better Betty Botter bought a bit of better butter.

Varying the voice

"*Vary your voice!*" is a favourite starting point on this theme in any book or seminar on presentation techniques. But how do we do this? After all, we are supposed to sound natural and authentic. Has anybody in normal life ever told you that your voice is too monotonous when you are talking about your favourite hobby or your family? Probably not, because the images you have in your head and the emotions that go with them lend colour to your speech. Actors will often use this phenomenon to good effect. A good actor should be able to read part of a phonebook out loud, without it becoming boring. Christoph Maria Herbst brought out a thrilling audiobook with sections from the German Civil Code. YouTube also carries examples of actors reading from phonebooks, such as Henry Cavill and Armie Hammer.

Alongside their speech technique, actors stimulate their imaginative abilities by visualizing what they are saying. Here is an example:

Franz Bauer
Holzweg 5
Ufenau, Germany

- What does this Franz Bauer fellow look like? How does he dress? How does he move, and smell? What does his voice sound like?
- What does Holzweg look like? Is it tarmac, or cobbles, or a gravel track? Are there many cars? Trees along the sides? How loud is it? . . .
- And Ufenau? How big is Ufenau, how does it feel, what does it sound like, what is the quality of the light, how far is it from the lake? And so on.

Figure 8.3 © Evi Fill

In Chekhov's "The Cherry Orchard," Anya says: "*On the way I did not sleep for four nights . . . Now I'm frozen to the core.*" An actor in this role must think about the reasons for which Anya has not slept for so long, what the train compartment was like, how she felt as the cold spread through her body, how the train smelled, and so on. Then, learning the text by heart becomes far easier.

We can, of course, practise this:

Exercise

Visualizing texts

Each participant is given a short text. In pairs, they read the text to each other. Next, they read it to themselves, and try to visualize it. Then they read it to each other again, and comment on any differences between the two readings.

For a presentation, this means keeping an image of what we are saying in our mind's eye. Here is an example:

"Our company strategy for 2018 is as follows:

*   International growth
*   Client orientation
*   Market leadership"

All these words are rather abstract, and need to be charged with meaning. Similarly hollow words are "synergy," "transparency," "sustainability," and so on. The questions below can help us give meaning to these words:

*   International growth: Which countries are we talking about? What are we selling there and to whom? What does this mean for staff?
*   Client orientation: Which clients do we mean? What does "orientation" look like?
*   Market leadership: Where do we currently stand compared to other companies? Who is the competition? How do we get there?

We should be able to answer these questions so that we know what we are talking about, and so that we can build images in our mind that will pep up our speech. We can even use these mental images to better describe the subject for our audience. (See the section on spoken images.)

Speech

Full stops in speech

In my seminars I frequently hear people running their sentences together with "and" or "er," and scarcely using a virtual full stop. The melody remains correspondingly level and monotonous, never dropping at the end of a sentence. Some people are worried about losing the thread; others cannot put the brakes on their flow of thoughts and words. But in both cases, the audience will quickly lose interest, as in the following example:

> *My name is Sabine Keller, I am 40 years old and I work as a customer adviser in a bank, er, well, I come from Frankfurt and now I live in Berlin and in my free time I like playing volleyball and do a lot of yoga, anyway in my presentation today I'm going to talk about . . .*

The short text above is lacking as many as four full stops:

> *My name is Sabine Keller. I am 40 years old and I work as a customer adviser in a bank. I come from Frankfurt and now I live in Berlin. In my free time I like playing volleyball, and I do a lot of yoga. In my presentation today I'm going to talk about . . .*

It helps to record ourselves and check how often we add a virtual full stop to our speech, often marked by a drop in tone.

Pauses

A full stop is an excellent chance for a pause. Pauses are as important to a presentation as the text itself, as it is in that moment of silence that the text will sink in. The text will only start to have an effect once there is a pause, and we must not disrupt the silence with filler words such as "er" and "so . . .."

There are essentially three types of pause: initial pause, transition pause, and dramatic pause (pause for effect). These three types of pause will probably be of different lengths, and should in any case vary.

Initial pause

As described above, we can immediately boost the impact of our presentation by pausing before we even begin.

Transition pause

Before each new section or idea, a transition pause is needed for what has just been said to have its effect, for the audience to process it, and for them to get ready for the next part.

Dramatic pauses

This type of pause is used to emphasize certain parts of what we say, and is also known as caesura, or pause for effect. Dramatic pauses raise the tension and the anticipation of what will come next. It is a good idea to think in advance about where to introduce these pauses, as in the following example:

> *My name is Robert Hauser. I'm a student of architecture, and I come from Vienna, from the second district. In the second district we also have Prater, a huge park in the middle of the city. I grew up just near there, and spent much of my childhood around Prater. **[Transition pause (short)]** When I was still a kid I started thinking about how to make this park even more exciting for children. That's why I'm studying architecture, **[Dramatic pause (longer)]** and it would be my dream project to remodel Prater.*

If we like to work with prompt notes, we can note these pauses down on the cards; for long pauses, we can even insert blank cards, so that the pause has to last at least as long as it takes to leaf through the cards.

Modal verbs and qualifiers

A clear and direct style of speech makes a presentation easier to understand. Modal verbs such as "may," "should," "could," and "would" also lower our status.

Other words that tend to weaken the effect of a message include qualifiers such as "somewhat," "a bit," "hopefully," "probably," "actually," and "possibly."

Using the I form

Which of the following phrases has the most effect?

> *He was very shaken by the experience.*
> *One is very shaken by such an experience.*
> *You would be very shaken by such an experience.*
> *I was very shaken by the experience.*

Presentations using "I" are more direct, and will connect with the audience better.

Images in words

While it is very important to have an excellent grasp of what we are talking about, and to be able to visualize it, we must also be able to communicate the subject matter itself to our audience vividly and understandably. This translation technique, particularly of abstract themes, may be termed "images in words."

Journalists attempt to package their texts as graphic ideas and stories, because they know that nobody is likely to voluntarily read dry business reports in their free time. Presenters will find that images in words are an excellent way to make themselves quickly and clearly understood by their audience. These images and stories are what remain in the memory, and will be talked about well after the event.

There are various ways to make any theme more vivid:

Verbal images

Verbal images are essentially metaphors (such as *"The sun rises when I look upon you."*), similes (*"You shine like the sun."*), or personifications (*"The sun is smiling."*).

Images

Images can be not only shown, but also narrated: *"Solar panels convert sunlight into energy for heating."*

A sentence like that may be understandable, but we still have difficulty picturing it.

> *When sunlight strikes a dark surface, it will warm that surface. Solar panels use this effect: they are made up of tubes containing fluid, which flows through the tubes, is warmed by the sun, and goes on to heat the entire house.*

Now we can more easily picture what is happening.

Examples

We can also use examples to shine light on abstract facts, by describing a typical case.

> *When sunlight strikes a dark surface, it will warm that surface. Solar panels use this effect. You can feel it yourself when you walk across a tarmac with bare feet on a sunny day.*

Meaningful images such as this lodge in our audience's memory more quickly, and will stay there longer.

Stories

> *Space scientists were the first to have the idea of using the sun to generate energy. They needed to find a way to provide electricity to satellites in space. As there are no electrical sockets up there, and since batteries will eventually run flat, they came up with the idea of using the rays of the sun to generate electricity. So the first solar energy equipment was built into satellites.*

Techniques for incorporating stories into presentations are covered in more detail in the chapter on "Storytelling."

Humour

"Good morning. My name is Susanne Schinko-Fischli. I originally come from Vienna, and 10 years ago I moved to the darkest reaches of Appenzell, after marrying a fellow from that area (a somewhat strange folk even by Swiss standards). These things can happen." This always gets a laugh in Switzerland, and I score a few points on the likeability scale. Being able to make fun of ourselves can make us approachable and personable, so it is essential that humour in a presentation should only be directed against ourselves. This type of humour fosters emotional transparency and authenticity in the eyes of the audience.

While we can to some extent plan humourous elements into our presentations to keep things relaxed, spontaneous humour will always be far more effective, because it is born out of our connection to the audience. As in improvisational theatre, this means avoiding unnecessarily blocking ourselves, and reacting spontaneously to the situation. Being funny is usually funniest when we are not always trying to be funny.

Humour can bring people together and help them overcome their differences, making it an essential tool in difficult situations. In his book *Improvised, Inc.* (2017, pp. 139–140), Robert Lowe describes an amusing event that happened to him:

> *I spoke to the professional development organization of a very large utility company. The evening dinner setting was outdoors by the pool of a fine hotel. I was to motivate and inspire the gathering. People were finishing dinner as I began to speak. There were some people not yet with me, so I searched for the words and gathered the energy that would allow the connection to become complete.*
>
> *Suddenly I felt something drop onto the top of my head. The people became silent and perfectly attendant. There was neither branch nor tree anywhere near, and the deep blue summer sky was cloudless. On my pant leg was the remains of the bird poop that had bounced off the top of my head. The gathering had become wonderfully focused . . . .*
>
> *Being in the Improvisation state of Impro, I grabbed a napkin, wiped the remains from my head, and said that I hoped it was not a comment on my message. There was a gentle, respectful laughter. I was a professional . . . . To this day I thank the bird. It brought us closer together. It made my serious message more real, more human, and more memorable. It demonstrated that I could laugh at myself.*

Figure 8.4 © Evi Fill

Humour works when four basic principles of improvisation are observed:

1   Be in the moment and keep your eyes open for what is happening around you – that is where you will find material for an amusing remark.
2   Say "Yes, and . . ." to your own and others' ideas – do not tie yourself down.
3   Let your partner/the audience look good – so that nobody is denigrated.
4   Have the self-control to avoid trying to be funny at all costs – as only then can things get really funny.

We can train our ability to say "Yes, and . . ." to our own ideas and impulses (see "Creativity" chapter), along with our spontaneity and ability to make associations.
   The following exercises are good examples:

Exercise

Creating associations

This requires two players. One says two words, and the other must make an association between them:

   Player A: "*Snow and love.*"
   Player B: "*Love can make it through the deepest snow*" or "*Love is like snow: light, flaky, and impermanent.*"

Exercise

Five things

The players stand in a circle. One player points at another and asks him a question, for example: *"Tell me five things you would like for Easter."* That player must then name five things as quickly as possible, which should not be true, but associative. Then the whole group calls out *"Five things!"*, and the player takes his turn to ask another player a new question, for example: *"Tell me five things you would never want to do."*

The whole game should be played fairly quickly, so that there is little time to think about either the questions or the answers.

The closing

The end of a presentation will ideally represent a kind of "closing bracket." Journalists talk about such stylistic devices, which aim to tie up the thread of a text by referring back to the beginning. Such a "bracket" will clearly indicate that the presentation has drawn to an end. For example, Dr Meier, our photovoltaics expert, might start and end his presentation as follows:

Start: *"Hello! My name is Heinrich Meier. I grew up in quite modest conditions on a farm in southern Germany. We used to have a lot of power cuts at home, and I still remember how inconvenient this was for our parents, who had to look after four of us kids . . ."*

End: *"Today, my parents' farm is a pioneer in the area of 'agricultural photovoltaics' – and furthermore has benefited from the reliability of energy supply to also become a pioneer in organic farming and diversity of species."*

Dealing with criticism

If we allow questions, interjections, and comments throughout a presentation, and if we explicitly request them during pauses, we can avoid a buildup of – potentially negative – feedback at the end. But even if time constraints restrict questions to the end of a presentation, any criticism must certainly not be countered with justifications – and most certainly not by insulting the person who gave the criticism. For example, at a presentation on the subject of status, we may have the following situation:

Audience member: *"I can't agree with anything you're saying about status. I am familiar with this term from sociology, where it has an entirely different meaning, and according to Ralph Linton's role theory social status corresponds to social position, and is not so easy to change as you claim."*

How would things turn out if the presenter answered as follows?

> *I can tell that you clearly haven't yet understood the concept of status. Obviously, what I'm doing here is intentionally contrasting this model against the static role models of other authors. The term "status" as used here was described by Keith Johnstone as something that a person "does," and is independent of social status, which is something that a person "has."*

It is unlikely that the person who asked the question is going to simply accept this, and the situation could easily develop into an unproductive and unpleasant argument. When criticism is in the air, the discussion – rather than leading to an interesting debate between different opinions – will often descend into personal posturing. The critic may want to make himself visible, to stand out from the anonymous mass of spectators. Indeed, the use of quotations and "clever" jargon can be an indicator of this. It is then important to give the critic space to make themselves seen, which can be made easier with an internalized "Yes, and . . .," that is, through receptive and accepting behaviour.

A better answer to the criticism above could be:

> *Indeed, status is understood to be many different things, and we can use the word in many different ways. Please tell us a little about the word "status" as applied in Ralph Linton's role model. I would be very interested to see if there was any connection between that and my own observations.*

We can see here that the spotlight shining on the presenter moves to the questioner/critic, directing the attention towards him for a while. This can be practised in a group with the following role-play:

Exercise

Dealing with criticism

A participant is given a subject about which he has just made a presentation (e.g. horses). He thanks the audience for listening, and invites questions:

> *I thank you for your attention, and will now take your questions.*

A member of the audience then asks a tricky question or makes a critical remark:

What you've just said in your talk is completely at odds with the latest scientific research!

The presenter now tries to address this question with an internalized "Yes, and . . .":

Ah, that's interesting. Which research do you mean?

The other participants, and particularly the critic, then give feedback on how the presenter dealt with the criticism.

Conclusion

A successful appearance in front of an audience brings together many elements described throughout this book. It is about being present, giving our full attention to the here and now, and not thinking ahead. And it is about saying "Yes, and . . ." to ourselves, to our own ideas, and to the audience. We also need status flexibility, that is, the ability to adapt our own status to the situation. And storytelling is essential to make the subject matter exciting, and so that what we say can lodge in our listeners' minds.

To sum up, for successful presentations we should pay attention to the following:

- Establish presence – the ability to be in the moment – as a foundation for any good presentation.
- Develop empathy, so that we can put ourselves in our audience's position.
- Personal and true "hero's journey" stories are an excellent way to start any presentation, as they strengthen the credibility and authenticity of the presenter.
- Interaction with the audience gets them involved and boosts their interest.
- Status should be set at an appropriate level for the target group concerned.
- Humour is useful for generating sympathy and emotional transparency.
- Visualizing images about the subject, offering examples, and telling stories all help our vocal delivery to be more dynamic, and make the subject matter easier to grasp and understand.

- To put power in our voices, we need good voice techniques, imagination, and the correct intention.
- Saying "Yes, and . . ." helps us deal with criticism.
- To calm our nerves, it helps to stay in the moment and, above all, perform, perform, perform!

Practical examples

"Presentation skills," Zurich University of Applied Sciences

Main points

Organization:
The Zurich University of Applied Sciences is one of the leading universities in Switzerland for applied sciences, carrying out research, and providing apprenticeships, higher education, and services.

Assignment:
Improving presentation skills for people preparing to move from team member roles to management and leadership in their subject.

Duration:
One day

Target group:
Participants in the module on "Moderation and Management of Challenging Meetings" at the Institut für Pflege.

Goals:
Participants were to . . .

- assess their presentation skills
- increase and deepen their awareness of their own personal resources
- receive supportive feedback
- exchange experiences and learn from one another
- find out more about their own status when communicating with other people, and how to adapt it as necessary
- professionalize their presence, their performance, and their charisma in front of groups
- enhance their ability to cope with unexpected situations

Initial situation and highlights

The Moderation and Management of Challenging Meetings module trains core competencies among care experts. By working with applied improvisation, the participants seek to improve their communicative and performance abilities.

Appearing before others always means taking a prominent stance to represent something. Some people experience no particular difficulty, but many find presentations and similar activities stressful and overwhelming. However, these highly qualified care operatives require a certain level of competence in how they appear before others, irrespective of their individual tendencies and talents.

During this one-day course, the participants would have stimulating personal experiences, learn how to augment their own resources, and pick up fundamental takeaway points on how to manage themselves in their daily work.

The subject of status is central to communication with residents, patients, colleagues, and superiors, and thus represented the main theme of the workshop. One exercise was as follows:

Exercice

Status ladder

Four players improvise a scene together. For example, three people may enter the room of a resident at the home. The resident is already present. All four players should form a status ladder. This may involve the resident being at the bottom of the ladder, with the lower status, and all others entering the room consecutively taking on somewhat higher status, with the last person assuming the highest of all. Or the scene can be played the other way around, with the resident assuming the highest status.

A variant is as follows:

> The participants enter the room one after the other, as before, but now the ladder must be worked out for itself. Each must seek out his own status, but at the end a clear ladder from 1 to 4 should result.

At the end, it is discussed whether the status ladder was clear for everyone to see, or whether there were some battles over status. It is also interesting to see, of course, how the person playing the resident felt in each situation. This exercise is very helpful for learning how to change status and adapt it to the setting. It also clearly shows how status games influence communication, and feedback helps identify which status behaviour facilitates communication.

Another important element of the workshop was that the participants briefly introduced themselves, and received feedback on how they did this.

Customer feedback from Sabin Bührer (Head of Studies MAS in Patient and Family Education)

The ability to advise and train patients and their relatives, along with representing the specialty in interprofessional teams are all principal tasks for any care expert. This means that presentation skills are essential to them.

This workshop gave the participants not only the chance to expand these competencies through direct experience with a variety of improvisation situations, but also to reflect on their own behaviour and how that influenced themselves and the group.

Reflection supports critical thinking, and is an important element of professional behaviour. It expands our limited perception, and the resulting awareness of certain behaviours enables us to modify them in the future.

This workshop allowed the participants to expand their professional abilities, which are so necessary to the central challenge of care, that is, to understand and address the whole person.

"Presentation Skills," FH Campus Vienna, University of Applied Sciences

---

Main points

Organization:
The FH Campus Vienna is Austria's largest university of applied sciences. A variety of departments offer a large range of undergraduate and postgraduate programmes and master's degrees, both as full-time and part-time courses.

Assignment:
Creating the opening module for the internal management curriculum on the subject of presentation skills.

Duration:
1.5 days

Target group:
All managers at the FH Campus Vienna

Goals:
Participants were to . . .

- learn how to recognize body language and use it more consciously
- reflect on their own status in communication with others, and learn how to modify this as necessary
- professionalize their presence, their performance, and their charisma in front of groups
- enhance their spontaneity and their ability to deal with unexpected situations

Initial situation and highlights

The aim of this management curriculum was to further develop in a professional manner the management abilities of staff at FH Campus Vienna. The management training consisted of five multi-day modules:

- Presentation skills
- Multifunctional teambuilding
- Management in troubled times
- Management in the academic context
- Leadership in times of change

Three levels were taken into account: the factual level (knowledge and cognition), the relationships level (behaviour and attitudes), and the organizational/structural level (context and culture). The first module of the curriculum, on presentation skills, largely worked with applied improvisation.

After introductory exercises on "Yes, and . . .," status, and storytelling, the focus moved to telling personal "hero's journey" stories, followed by a video analysis:

Exercise

Hero's journey

The participants prepared a personal hero's journey story, and presented it in their own entirely individual way. The story had to be true, and the storyteller had to be the hero, in the sense that they had overcome extensive personal challenges in their life, and had integrated what they had learned into their personality.

Given that the participants already had significant experience with presentations, I decided to turn up the heat by asking them to bring in personal stories from their own lives. These should illustrate difficult situations, and relate how they had faced these situations, and what they had learned from them.

To this end, I suggested the following:

- How did you decide what to study, and what to make your profession?
- How did you come to FH Campus Vienna?
- Are there any other challenging situations in your personal life that have also affected your professional life?

The presentations were videoed and analysed together. We particularly looked at the extent to which the stories were appropriate for the target group, how they were compiled, and how the arc of tension was formed. Naturally, we also looked at elements of presentation skills: status, body language, speech, voice, pauses, and so on.

This exercise also had a teambuilding effect. Even though the participants already knew each other well, they were still able to find out new things about each other.

Customer feedback from Birgit Matthaei (Head of Personnel Management)

We chose the module "Presentation Skills" as the opener for a comprehensive training curriculum offered to all managers at FH Campus Vienna.

As most of the participants already had a lot of experience in presentations and public speaking, we thought it was important to use creative and original methods that would be surprising and offer new perspectives. We also wanted the module to have a teambuilding effect, and weld together the managers as a learning group for the rest of the curriculum.

The module achieved all this exceptionally well. This was largely down to the great variety of exercises from applied improvisation, and the experience of the trainer in her subject and working with it in groups.

It was certainly a successful and enjoyable start to the curriculum, which provided much opportunity for participants to learn more about themselves. It also bonded the group together as we had hoped, which was an excellent basis for the success of the subsequent modules.

Exercises for presentation skills

1   Arc of Tension

Procedure: One person delivers a presentation, or tells a story. Members of the audience lift their hands when the tension starts to diminish. The presenter thus receives direct feedback on the arc of tension in the presentation or story.

Themes:

> **Presence:** Only through our presence can we convince our audience and hold their attention. This exercise clearly indicates whether we have this presence.
>
> **Building tension:** This exercise helps us learn how to build tension slowly, and how to maintain it throughout the presentation.
>
> **Arc of tension:** The audience members' hands show us immediately if our presentation or story is still interesting.

2 Ask a Stupid Question

Procedure: Two players ask each other stupid questions, such as *"What does an elephant wear in bed?"* The other player must answer as quickly as possible.

Themes:

> **Creativity:** This exercise requires us to spontaneously come up with creative questions and answers.

3 Call-out Presentation

Procedure: The participant is given a subject by the audience, and has to start talking about it spontaneously. Audience members then call out words, and the presenter must incorporate them immediately into their presentation.

Themes:

> **Spontaneity:** Building called-out words into a presentation as quickly as possible simulates coping with spontaneous interjections in a real presentation.

4 Colour and Advance

Procedure: This exercise requires two players. One begins to deliver a short presentation, or invents a story. At any moment the other player can say *"Colour,"* at which point the presenter must describe a person or object from the story in greater detail, until the observer says *"Advance,"* whereby the main presentation or story may continue.

Themes:

> **Compiling stories:** We learn to recognize when to push the story forward, and when we should go into more detail.

5 Creating Associations

Procedure: This requires two players. One says two words, and the other must make an association between them:

Player A: *"Snow and love."*

Player B: *"Love can make it through the deepest snow"* or *"Love is like snow: light, flaky, and impermanent."*

Themes:

> **Spontaneity:** This exercise helps us practise spontaneity as a basis for humour.

6 Dealing with Criticism

Procedure: A participant is given a subject about which he has just made a presentation (e.g. horses). He thanks the audience for listening, and invites questions. A member of the audience then asks a tricky question or makes a critical remark. The presenter now tries to address this question with an internalized "Yes, and . . ." The other participants, and particularly the critic, then give feedback on how the presenter dealt with the criticism.

Themes:

> **Accepting offers:** The players learn how to react to criticism with an internal "Yes, and . . ."

7   Five Things

Procedure: The players stand in a circle. One player points at another and asks him a question, for example: "*Tell me five things you would like for Easter.*" That player must then name five things as quickly as possible, which should not be true, but associative. Then the whole group calls out "*Five things!*", and the player takes his turn to ask another player a new question, for example: "*Tell me five things you would never want to do.*" The whole game should be played fairly quickly, so that there is little time to think about either the questions or the answers.

Themes:

> **Spontaneity:** Another exercise to practise spontaneity.
>
> **Association:** We can use this exercise to learn rapid association.

8   Glorious Presentation

Procedure: Everyone stands in a circle, and introduces their neighbour to make them appear as majestic and wonderful as possible, using made-up devices such as "*Lucas's eyes can melt the snow. With eyes like his, he can . . . .*"

Themes:

> **Spontaneity:** Players must be able to come up with something on the spot.
>
> **Teamwork:** The group will bond together more strongly, because each member has something positive said about them.

9   Half-time Presentation

Procedure: The presenter must deliver her talk in half the original time, then in half the time again, and so on until only the very most important elements remain.

Themes:

> **Boiling down to the essential:** Here, we are forced to concentrate more and more on the essential elements, until at the end we are only saying what is absolutely most important.

10   PowerPoint Karaoke

Procedure: The participants are given a randomly chosen PowerPoint presentation that they have never seen before, and must make a presentation based on it, which they make up on the spot.

Themes:

> **Spontaneity:** The players use the slides to talk about a subject they have little knowledge of.

Storytelling: This works best when people make up stories around the subject, or tell a true story related to it. All this depends on how quickly a person can make links between their own existing knowledge and experience, and the subject they have been given.

11 Presence Exercise

Procedure: One player stands before the audience (without speaking or doing anything). As soon as a member of the audience becomes bored, that person should raise his hand. When more than half of the audience has raised their hands, the exercise is over.

Themes:

Presence: How long can we hold the audience's attention without speaking?

12 Visualizing Texts

Procedure: Each participant is given a short text. In pairs, they read the text to each other. Next, they read it to themselves, and try to visualize it. Then they read it to each other again, and comment on any differences between the two readings.

Themes:

Developing mental images: The participants learn how to develop mental images, to bring more life and colour to their vocal delivery.

13 Waiting at the Start

Procedure: A person stands before the group, as if at the start of a presentation, and says nothing. Those watching him raise their hand once they begin to feel bored. This is usually a lot later than the presenter himself would imagine.

Themes:

Initial pause: This exercise helps us tolerate the silence of an initial pause at the start, and to judge how long such a pause should be.

Status exercises for presentations

1 High Status/Low Status

Procedure: Audience members can do this with their neighbour. They should introduce themselves, first using high status (e.g. a long firm handshake, maintaining eye contact all the time), then low status (e.g. a limp handshake, scarcely making eye contact). At the end, they should talk about how they perceived the differences between the two greetings.

Themes:

Status: The exercise offers our first experience of high- and low-status behaviour.

2 I am the Director

Procedure: One participant leaves the room, then comes back in through the door as the director/CEO of the company/university etc., and greets everyone in the room while playing this role.

Themes:

Status flexibility: Here we learn how to raise our status.

3   **Status Feedback**

Procedure: A player comes on stage and tries to stand as "neutrally" as possible. Members of the audience call out a number from 1 to 10 according to what level of status they perceive in the player on stage. If desired, feedback may also be given as to how these evaluations were arrived at, that is, which signals and body language had the effect of raising or lowering the player's status.

Themes:

Status sensitivity: We can use this exercise to sharpen our awareness for our own status.

4   **Status Ladder**

Procedure: Four players improvise a scene together (e.g. colleagues having a drink after work). They come on stage one after the other, with each person assuming a status somewhat higher than those already present.

Variant: The players must find their place on the status ladder, status level 1–4, without the order being specified first.

Themes:

Status sensitivity: The players must be able to recognize the status of their counterparts.

Status flexibility: They must be able to adapt their status to the others' status.

5   **Status Presentation**

Procedure: One player comes on stage, and a number from 1 to 10 is whispered in her ear (1 is the lowest status, 10 the highest). The player must then come to the centre of the stage and announce, "*Good evening, ladies and gentlemen,*" using the status level that was whispered to her. The audience must then guess which number she was given.

Themes:

Status sensitivity: This exercise helps us recognize high-status and low-status signals.

Status flexibility: We learn to modify our status by adapting it to the numbers we are given.

Voice and breathing exercises

1   **Abdominal Breathing Alone**

Procedure: Place one hand on your stomach and the other on the upper part of your chest. At first, breathe normally, and feel how your hands move. If the upper hand moves more, this is chest breathing. Now concentrate on directing the breathing deep into the abdomen, towards the other hand. The belly should then move outwards, indicating abdominal breathing.

Themes:

> **Abdominal breathing:** This exercise lets us experience abdominal breathing.

2   **Breathing Control**

Procedure: Stand upright, hands on hips. Pronounce a series of consonants loudly: "t, k, f, s, . . ." You should be able to feel the movement of the diaphragm as far down as the hips. After each consonant, the stomach moves inwards, then outwards to draw air into the lungs. The body inhales the air that it needs. This exercise can also be done with short words, such as "hey" or "stop," as if you were calling out to someone.

Themes:

> **Controlled breathing:** This exercise helps us train our breathing control.

3   **Breathing Exercise with Another Person**

Procedure: Person A stands squarely on both feet. Person B moves around him and places her hands on various parts of his torso. Person A attempts to direct his breathing towards her hands. Then they discuss how it felt for Person A. Where could he "place" his breathing? Where did Person B feel it?

Themes:

> **Awareness of our own breathing:** This exercise increases our awareness of our breath.

4   **Cork Exercise**

Procedure: Each participant is given a cork (or, even better, they use their thumb). Then, in pairs, they read a short text out loud with the cork or their thumb in their mouth, and then without. Each then comments on whether the other's pronunciation improved after using the cork.

Themes:

> **Pronunciation:** This exercise is excellent for improving the clarity of our pronunciation in a short time.

5   **Paper on the Wall**

Procedure: Take a small sheet of paper and hold it against the wall at the level of your mouth. Stand around 20 cm back, and place your other hand on your stomach. Then let go of the paper and try to hold it against the wall by blowing it steadily. Your stomach should feel resistant to your hand. The longer you can hold the paper against the wall, the better you are already controlling your breathing.

Themes:

> **Controlled breathing:** We experience how breathing can be controlled.

Bibliography

Alter, J. (2006). *The defining moment: FDR's hundred days and the triumph of hope.* New York: Simon & Schuster Paperbacks.

Aristoteles. (1999). *Rhetorik.* Translated and published by Gernot Krapinger. Stuttgart: Reclam Verlag.

Gallo, C. (2009). *The presentation secrets of Steve Jobs: How to be insanely great in front of any audience.* New York: McGraw-Hill Education Ltd.

Jobs, S. (2007). *I-Phone Key Note – 9.1.2007.* San Francisco: MacWorld.

Lowe, R. (2017). *Improvised, Inc.* Atlanta: RLJ Publications.

Bibliography

Adams, K. (2007). *How to improvise a full-length play – The art of spontaneous theater.* New York: Allworth.

Alter, J. (2006). *The defining moment: FDR's hundred days and the triumph of hope.* New York: Simon & Schuster Paperbacks.

Aristoteles. (1999). *Rhetorik.* Translated and published by Gernot Krapinger. Stuttgart: Reclam Verlag.

Backera, H., Malorny, C., and Schwarz, W. (2007). *Kreativitätstechniken.* Munich: Hanser.

Basadur, M. (1994). *Simplex: A flight to creativity.* Canada: The Creative Education Foundation.

Bischof, N. (2004). *Das Kraftfeld der Mythen. Signale aus der Zeit, in der wir die Welt erschaffen haben.* Munich: Piper.

Bono, E. de. (1970). *Lateral thinking.* London: Penguin.

Bonsen, M. (2000). Eine neue Geschichte erzählen: Spirit, Mythen, Großgruppen-Interventionen und liturgische Systeme. In: Königswieser, R. and Keil, M. (Pub.), *Das Feuer großer Gruppen, Konzepte, Designs, Praxisbeispiele für Großveranstaltungen* (pp. 85–99). Stuttgart: Klett-Cotta.

Cossart, E. V. (2017). *Story tells – Story sells.* 3nd edn. Bergisch-Gladbach: Lesedrehbuch .

Csíkszentmihályi, M. (1996). *Creativity: Flow and the psychology of discovery and invention.* New York: Harper Perennial.

Dixon, R. (2000). *Im Moment – Theaterkunst Improvisationstheater, Reflexionen und Perspektiven.* Planegg: Impuls Buschfunk.

Edmondson, A. (2013). *Teaming to innovate.* San Francisco: Bass & Wiley.

Engelke, E. (1981). *Psychodrama in der Praxis.* Munich: Pfeiffer.

Esslin, M. (1978). *Was ist ein Drama?* Munich: Piper.

Esslin, M. (1989). *Die Zeichen des Dramas. Theater. Film. Fernsehen.* Reinbek bei Hamburg: Rowohlt.

Field, S. (1991). *Das Handbuch zum Drehbuch.* Frankfurt a. M.: Zweitausendeins.

Frenzel, K., Müller, M., and Sottong, H. (2004). *Storytelling. Das Harun-al-Raschid-Prinzip. Die Kraft des Erzählens fürs Unternehmen nutzen.* Munich: Hanser.

Frenzel, K., Müller, M., and Sottong, H. (2006). *Storytelling – das Praxisbuch.* Munich: Carl Hanser.

Freytag, G. (1972). *Die Technik des Dramas.* 2nd edn. Leipzig: Hirzel.

Fuchs, W. T. (2015). *Warum das Gehirn Geschichten liebt.* 3rd edn. Freiburg: Haufe-Lexware.

Funcke, A. and Havermann-Feye, M. (2004). *Training mit Theater*. Bonn: managerSeminare.

Gallo, C. (2009). *The presentation secrets of Steve Jobs: How to be insanely great in front of any audience*. New York: McGraw-Hill Education Ltd.

Goddard, P. (2015). *Improving agile teams*. Bradford on Avon: Agilify.

Goergens, S. F. (2009). *Brainstorming – Irren ist quantitativ*. München: Focus 05.

Goethe, J. W. (2009, 1795). *Wilhelm Meisters Lehrjahre*. Frankfurt a. M. and Leipzig: Insel.

Halpern, C., Close, D., and Johnson, H. K. (1994). *Truth in comedy – The manual of improvisation*. Colorado Springs: Meriwether.

Haslam, A., Adarves-Yorno, I., Postmes, T., and Jans, L. (2013). The collective origins of valued originality – A social identity approach to creativity. *Personality and Social Psychology Review*, 17, 384–401.

Hesse, H. (1974, 1919). *Demian*. Frankfurt a. M.: Suhrkamp.

Jackson, P. Z. (2015). *Easy – Your lifepass to creativity and confidence*. London: The Solution Focus.

Jobs, S. (2007). *I-Phone Key Note – 9.1.2007*. San Francisco: MacWorld.

Johnstone, K. (1981). *Improvisation and the theatre*. 2nd edn. London: Methuen Paperback.

Johnstone, K. (1999). *Impro for Storytellers*. 2nd edn. London: Routledge.

Kast, B. (2015). *Klick! Das Handwerk der Kreativität oder wie die guten Ideen in den Kopf kommen*. Frankfurt a. M.: Fischer.

Keefe, J. (2003). *Improv yourself – Business spontaneity at the speed of thought*. Hoboken: Wiley.

Kelley, T. and Littman, J. (2001). *The art of innovation – Lessons in creativity from IDEO, America's leading design firm*. London: Bookmarque.

Kolb, D. A. (1984). *Experiential learning – Experience as the source of learning and development*. Upper Saddle River: Prentice Hall.

Koppett, K. (2001). *Training to imagine – Practical improvisational theatre techniques to enhance creativity, teamwork, leadership and learning*. Sterling: Stylus.

Kruse, O. (1997). *Kreativität als Ressource für Veränderung und Wachstum*. Tübingen: Deutsche Gesellschaft für Verhaltenstherapie.

Kruse, P. (2004). *Next practice – Erfolgreiches Management von Instabilität*. Offenbach: Gabal.

Lehner, J. M. and Ötsch, W. O. (2015). *Jenseits der Hierarchie – Status im beruflichen Alltag aktiv gestalten*. 2nd edn. Weinheim: Wiley-VCH.

Leonard, K. and Yorton, T. (2015). *Yes, and – Lessons from the second city*. New York: Collins.

Lösel, G. (2004). *Theater ohne Absicht – Impulse zur Weiterentwicklung des Improvisationstheaters*. Planegg: Impuls Buschfunk.

Lowe, R. (2017). *Improvised, Inc*. Atlanta: RLJ Publications.

Luft, J. (1963). *Einführung in die Gruppendynamik*. Stuttgart: Klett.

Masemann, S. and Messer, B. (2009). *Improvisation und Storytelling in Training und Unterricht*. Weinheim and Basel: Beltz.

McDreadie, D. (2014). *You will never be funny*. 2nd edn. Poland: Amazon.

Moreno, J. L. (1924). *Das Stegreiftheater*. Potsdam: des Vaters. Kiepenheuer.

Mück, F. (2016). *Der einfache Weg zum begeisternden Vortrag*. 2nd edn. Munich: Redline-Verlag.

Müller, M. (2007). Storytelling: die Wiederentdeckung des narrativen Denkens in Unternehmen. *Wirtschaftspsychologie aktuell*, 2.

Nachmanovitch, S. (1990). *Free play – Improvisation in life and art*. New York: Penguin Putnam.

Paolini, C. P. (2004–2011). *Eragon*. New York: Random House.

Paris, V. and Bunse, M. (1994). *Improvisationstheater mit Kindern und Jugendlichen*. Reinbek bei Hamburg: Rowohlt.

Rowling, J. K. (1997–2007). *Harry Potter*. London: Bloomsbury.

Rustler, F. (2016). *Denkwerkzeuge der Kreativität und Innovation*. St. Gallen and Zurich: Midas Management.

Salinsky, T. and Frances-White, D. (2010). *The improv handbook*. New York: Continuum.

Schank, R. C. (2000). *Tell me a story: Narrative and intelligence*. 3rd edn. Evanston: Northwestern University.

Schmitt, T. and Esser, M. (2012). *Status Spiele – Wie ich in jeder Situation die Oberhand behalte*. Frankfurt a. M.: Fischer.

Schreyögg, G. and Dabitz, R. (1999). *Unternehmenstheater*. Wiesbaden: Gabler.

Schuler, H. and Görlich, Y. (2007). *Kreativität*. Göttingen: Hogrefe.

Schwarz, G. (2003). *Konfliktmanagement*. Wiesbaden: Gabler & GWV.

Senge, P. (1997). *Die fünfte Disziplin*. Stuttgart: Klett-Cotta.

Simanowitz, J. (2016). *Performance coaching – Kreative Rollen- und Statusspiele im Job*. Weinheim and Basel: Beltz.

Spitzer, M. (2002). *Lernen – Gehirnforschung und die Schule des Lebens*. Berlin: Spektrum.

Spolin, V. (1963). *Improvisation for the theater*. Chicago: Northwestern University Press.

Thier, K. (2017). *Storytelling – Eine Methode für das Change-, Marken- und Projektmanagement*. 3rd edn. Berlin and Heidelberg: Springer.

Thöneböhn, S. (2006). *Geschichten des Augenblicks, Struktur und Dramaturgie im Improvisationstheater am Beispiel der Heldenreise*. Magisterarbeit: Leibnitz Universität Hannover.

Tiggeler, N. (2016). *Mit Stimme zum Erfolg*. Munich: Verlag C.H. Beck.

Tolkien, J. R. R. (2007, 1945–1955). *The lord of the rings*. London: Harper Collins Publisher.

Tschechow, A. (Checkov, A.) (1984). *Der Kirschgarten*. Stuttgart: Philipp Reclam jun. GmbH & Co. KG.

Vlcek, R. (2002). *Workshop Improvisations theater*. Donauwörth: Auer.

Vogler, C. (2007). *The writer's journey: Mythic structure for writers*. 3rd edn. Chelsea: Sheridan.

Wallas, G. (1926). *The art of thought*. Kent: Solis.

Zaporah, R. (1995). *Action theatre: The improvisation of presence*. Berkeley: North Atlantic Books.

Zenk, L. (2012). *Team-Kreativität: Innovation durch improvisation*. Working Paper, Vienna.

Online sources

The Applied Improvisation Network. Available at: http://appliedimprovisation.network/about-applied-improvisation/ [Accessed 29 May 2018].

Beglinger, M. (2013). Der Staat der Physiker (Cern). *Das Magazin*. Available at: www.dasmagazin.ch/2013/10/25/der-staat-der-physiker/?reduced=true [Accessed 29 May 2018].

Boyke, G. (2015). Improgruppen weltweit. *Improwiki*. Available at: https://improwiki. com/de/liste_improgruppen_weltweit [Accessed 12 July 2018].

Boyke, G. (2015). Status. *Improwiki*. Available at: http://improwiki.com/de/wiki/ improtheater/status [Accessed 29 May 2018].

Bussmann, N. (2012). Trainingsmethoden 2012: Shooting Star Storytelling. *ManagerSeminare.de*. Available at: https://managerseminare.de/blog/trainingsmethoden-2012-shooting-star-storytelling/2012/07 [Accessed 12 July 2018].

Chors, C. (2016). Der Mann, der im Niemandsland am schnellsten E-Auto der Welt tüftelt. *Stern*. Available at: www.stern.de/auto/elektroautos-von-mate-rimac-elon-musk-des-balkans-6740858.html [Accessed 29 May 2018].

Duhigg, C. (2016). What google learned from its quest to build the perfect team. *The New York Times Magazine*. Available at: www.nytimes.com/2016/02/28/magazine/what-google-learned-from-its-quest-to-build-the-perfect-team.html?_r=0 [Accessed 29 May 2018].

Knauß, F. (2013). Genies sind keine Einzelgänger. *Wirtschaftswoche*. Available at: www. wiwo.de/erfolg/trends/kreativitaet-genies-sind-keine-einzelgaenger/8946456.html [Accessed 29 May 2018].

Lindner, K. (2011). 100 Jahre IBM – Beständigkeit durch Veränderung. *FAZ*. Available at: www.faz.net/aktuell/technik-motor/cebit-2011/100-jahre-ibm-bestaendigkeit-durch-veraenderung-1590277.html [Accessed 29 May 2018].

Tint, B. and Froerer, A. (2014). Delphi study summary. *Applied improvisation network*. Available at: http://appliedimprovisation.network/wp-content/uploads/2015/11/Delphi-Study-Summary.pdf [Accessed 29 May 2018].

Index

Note: Page numbers in *italic* indicate a figure and page numbers in **bold** indicate a table on the corresponding page.

For Product Safety Concerns and Information please contact our EU
representative GPSR@taylorandfrancis.com
Taylor & Francis Verlag GmbH, Kaufingerstraße 24, 80331 München, Germany

www.ingramcontent.com/pod-product-compliance
Lightning Source LLC
Chambersburg PA
CBHW050648280326
41932CB00015B/2826

9 781138 315266